Arsenal

PREMIERSHIP PLAYER PROFILES

AN OFFICIAL ARSENAL PUBLICATION

hamlyn

Arsenal

PREMIERSHIP PLAYER PROFILES

Chas Newkey-Burden

AN OFFICIAL ARSENAL PUBLICATION

FIRST PUBLISHED IN GREAT BRITAIN IN 2007 BY HAMLYN,
A DIVISION OF OCTOPUS PUBLISHING GROUP LTD
2–4 HERON QUAYS, LONDON E14 4JP

COPYRIGHT © OCTOPUS PUBLISHING GROUP LTD 2007
TEXT COPYRIGHT © OCTOPUS PUBLISHING GROUP LTD 2007

ISBN-13: 978-0-600-61680-1

A CIP CATALOGUE RECORD OF THIS BOOK IS AVAILABLE
FROM THE BRITISH LIBRARY.

PRINTED AND BOUND IN SLOVENIA

10 9 8 7 6 5 4 3 2 1

ABOUT THE STATISTICS
ALL STATISTICS ARE CORRECT UP TO THE END OF THE 2006/07 SEASON.
'APPEARANCES' REFERS TO COMPETITIVE MATCHES PLAYED FOR THE
CLUB AND 'OTHER HONOURS' COVERS FULL CAPS WON FOR THE PLAYERS'
NATIONAL SIDES. OTHER CLUBS LISTED IN PLAYERS' RECORDS ARE THOSE
LEAGUE CLUBS IN ENGLAND OR OVERSEAS FOR WHOM THE PLAYER HAS
PLAYED IN A FIRST-TEAM MATCH.

THE PERIODS GIVEN FOR ARSENAL PLAYERS' CAREERS COMMENCE
WITH THE SEASON IN WHICH THE PLAYER MADE HIS ARSENAL FIRST-TEAM
DEPUT, AND END WITH THE SEASON IN WHICH OR AFTER WHICH THE
PLAYER SIGNED FULL-TIME WITH ANOTHER CLUB OR RETIRED FROM
THE GAME.

CONTENTS

FOREWORD	6
DAVID O'LEARY	8
PAUL DAVIS	9
TONY ADAMS	10
PAUL MERSON	12
PERRY GROVES	14
JOHN LUKIC	15
MARTIN KEOWN	16
STEVE BOULD	18
KEVIN CAMPBELL	20
COLIN PATES	21
THE 100 CLUB!	22
NIGEL WINTERBURN	24
ANDY LINIGHAN	26
DAVID HILLIER	27
LEE DIXON	28
DAVID SEAMAN	30
ALAN SMITH	32
HIGH FIVES!	34
RAY PARLOUR	36
STEVE MORROW	38
JOHN JENSEN	39
ANDERS LIMPAR	40
NEIL HEANEY	42
JIMMY CARTER	42
PAL LYDERSEN	43
ALAN MILLER	43
IAN WRIGHT	44
PERFECT PARTNERSHIPS	46
GAVIN MCGOWAN	48
MARK FLATTS	48
VINCE BARTRAM	49
IAN SELLEY	49
PAUL DICKOV	50
SCOTT MARSHALL	50
EDDIE MCGOLDRICK	51
STEFAN SCHWARZ	52
JOHN HARTSON	53
CHRIS KIWOMYA	54
GLENN HELDER	55
STEPHEN HUGHES	56
PAUL SHAW	57
ADRIAN CLARKE	57
MATTHEW ROSE	58
LEE HARPER	58

REMI GARDE	59
DENNIS BERGKAMP	60
THE ROLL OF HONOUR	62
DAVID PLATT	64
NICOLAS ANELKA	66
WORLD-CLASS GUNNERS!	68
PATRICK VIEIRA	70
GILLES GRIMANDI	72
CHRISTOPHER WREH	73
EMMANUEL PETIT	74
MATTHEW UPSON	76
LUIS BOA MORTE	77
MARC OVERMARS	78
ALBERTO MENDEZ	80
PAOLO VERNAZZA	80
DAVID GRONDIN	81
FABIAN CABALLERO	81
ALEX MANNINGER	82
ISAIAH RANKIN	83
IGORS STEPANOVS	83
FREDRIK LJUNGBERG	84
NELSON VIVAS	86
SILVINHO	87
NWANKWO KANU	88
OLEG LUZHNY	90
STEFAN MALZ	91
KABA DIAWARA	91
CULT HEROES	92
THIERRY HENRY	94
JERMAINE PENNANT	96
DAVOR SUKER	97
EDU	98
ASHLEY COLE	100
GRAHAM BARRETT	102
RHYS WESTON	102
JULIAN GRAY	103
BRIAN MCGOVERN	103
ROBERT PIRES	104
DAVID BENTLEY	106
STUART TAYLOR	107
SYLVAIN WILTORD	108
RICHARD WRIGHT	110
TOMAS DANILEVICIUS	111
TOMMY BLACK	111
RYAN GARRY	111
LAUREN	112
PLANET ARSENAL	114

SOL CAMPBELL	116
GIOVANNI VAN BRONCKHORST	118
FRANCIS JEFFERS	119
GILBERTO	120
JEREMIE ALIADIERE	122
PASCAL CYGAN	123
THE INVINCIBLES!	124
KOLO TOURE	126
STATHIS TAVLARIDIS	128
RAMI SHAABAN	128
KERREA GILBERT	129
QUINCY OWUSU-ABEYIE	129
GAEL CLICHY	130
PHILIPPE SENDEROS	131
JENS LEHMANN	132
JOHAN DJOUROU	134
MATHIEU FLAMINI	135
FRANCESC FABREGAS	136
SEBASTIAN LARSSON	138
ARTURO LUPOLI	138
MANUEL ALMUNIA	139
THE HOME BOYS	140
JUSTIN HOYTE	142
JOSE ANTONIO REYES	143
ROBIN VAN PERSIE	144
EMMANUEL ADEBAYOR	146
EMMANUEL EBOUE	148
ALEXANDER HLEB	149
TOMAS ROSICKY	150
ABOU DIABY	151
THEO WALCOTT	152
WILLIAM GALLAS	154
TEEN SPIRIT	156
JULIO BAPTISTA	158
MART POOM	158
ALEXANDRE SONG	159
DENILSON	159
GEORGE GRAHAM	160
BRUCE RIOCH	162
STEWART HOUSTON	164
PAT RICE	165
ARSÈNE WENGER	166
CLUB RECORDS	168
PLAYER STATISTICS	170
INDEX	173
ACKNOWLEDGEMENTS	176

FOREWORD BY ARSÈNE WENGER

I have managed Arsenal for over ten years and have seen many great Premiership players. The quality of this League is so high, that only the very best footballers can succeed. The Premiership has showcased some of the world's most talented players and I feel lucky to have been given the opportunity to have managed such a successful team during this time.

F or any player, it is a great achievement to play in the Premiership, even if it is only for a few games. The speed of the Premiership and technical awareness of the players who play within it, set the Premier League aside from any other league in the world. These qualities, along with the passion and dedication of the players and fans, make the Premiership very special.

This is why I feel it is important that this book features every single footballer who has played for us in the Premiership. Some of them may have only played a few Premiership matches for us but they deserve their place in any Arsenal book. To highlight the quality of Arsenal throughout the Premiership years, we see that players like Jermaine Pennant, Matthew Upson and Luis Boa Morte, who only played a limited amount of games for us, have been able to forge successful careers at other top flight Clubs. Even those players who have been part of the squad during the Premiership years, perhaps only playing in Cup ties, have performed a crucial role for us behind the scenes as part of the Arsenal family.

Arsenal have been a dominant force in the Premiership since it began in 1992 and there have been many wonderful players who have pulled on the famous red and white shirt during this time. When I took over as manager in 1996, I was lucky enough to have inherited the famous back four who had played so well under

George Graham. Tony Adams, Lee Dixon, Nigel Winterburn and Steve Bould – along with Martin Keown, too – formed an amazing defensive unit, and I have often said that they were professors in the art of defending. I doubt that the Premiership will ever see a better group of defenders who could read the game so effectively as them. Now a young group of defenders are hoping to follow in their footsteps, including Kolo Toure, Gael Clichy, Emmanuel Eboue, Philippe Senderos, Johan Djourou and Justin Hoyte. I have every confidence that this group of immensely talented players can help to secure many future successes for the Club.

Crucially important to any defence is the goalkeeper. Again, I was lucky enough to have inherited a goalkeeper of the highest quality in David Seaman. He played a huge part in Arsenal's success and was at the top of the game for a long time. Replacing a goalkeeper like David is always tough. A lot of expectations rest on the shoulders of the new player. When I brought in Jens Lehmann, it was beyond my own expectations that this goalkeeper would help Arsenal secure the Premiership trophy in an unbeaten league season!

In midfield, some of the world's best have worn Arsenal colours. I remember watching Anders Limpar play before I joined Arsenal and I appreciated his intelligence and speed. He is certainly a player I would have liked to have

worked with. From George Graham's squad, I inherited great midfield talent including David Platt, Ray Parlour and Paul Merson. Since then, I have enjoyed watching the likes of Patrick Vieira, Emmanuel Petit, Robert Pires, Freddie Ljungberg and Gilberto, amongst others, play for Arsenal. All of these players have been very important in the continuing success of the Club. Equally important is the emerging midfield talent we now have. Cesc Fabregas, well known on the international stage as well as within our league, alongside Abou Diaby and Denilson are all still very young, but I know they have the talent and drive to succeed in the Premiership.

And finally, up front. When I arrived at Arsenal, I was looking forward to working with two of the greatest players the Club has ever seen. Ian Wright was already a goal-scoring legend and Dennis Bergkamp was world-renowned for his exquisite vision and technique. With this partnership up front, I was always confident we would score some goals! They also helped to raise the Club profile and made it easier to attract talent. In the Double winning season of 2007–08, I brought in Nicolas Anelka, who I still believe to be one of the best finishers in the game. Since then I have had the good fortune to manage some of the most technically-gifted forwards in the game, including Kanu, Sylvain Wiltord and of course, Thierry Henry. Thierry was not only a great player, but also a great character who was much loved by the Club and fans. Looking forward, I am excited to see how the current crop of young stars progress. Theo Walcott, Robin van Persie and Emmanuel Adebayor have the potential to become world-class strikers and three of the most feared players in the league.

The list of fantastic footballers who have played in the Arsenal shirt during the Premiership years goes on and on. This book highlights all of the Premiership players who have helped make this club as successful as it is now. I hope that you enjoy reading about them.

Arsène Wenger

DAVID O'LEARY

DAVID O'LEARY (1975/76–1992/93)	**CLUB HONOURS:** LEAGUE CHAMPIONSHIP 1989, 1991; FA CUP 1979, 1993; LEAGUE CUP 1987, 1993
POSITION: DEFENDER	
APPEARANCES: 722	**OTHER HONOURS:** 68 REPUBLIC OF IRELAND CAPS (1 GOAL)
GOALS: 14	
BORN: STOKE NEWINGTON, LONDON, 2 MAY 1958	**OTHER CLUBS:** LEEDS UNITED
	MANAGERIAL CAREER: LEEDS UNITED, ASTON VILLA

The Irishman saw Arsenal into the Premiership era, completed the cup double, then moved to Leeds United. He has since become a manager.

When the Premiership came into being, just 12 months of David O'Leary's Arsenal career remained and the Irishman had long since seen his best days in an Arsenal shirt. But how typical of this Gunners legend that even in his final season, he helped the Club to another two trophies and ended his Arsenal career by walking back down the steps at Wembley with an FA Cup winners' medal in his hand.

His Arsenal tenure straddled three decades and by the time he left Highbury, O'Leary waved goodbye to a squad that included players who were not born when he had first signed up with Arsenal. Such loyalty was not exactly commonplace then; now it is almost unheard of.

Hang around that long at Arsenal and you are odds-on to collect medals; he won two League Championships, two FA Cups and two League cups. Strong and fast, O'Leary was also a cultured player, particularly by the standards of centre backs in his era. He anticipated trouble a few crucial moments before anyone else did.

PAUL DAVIS

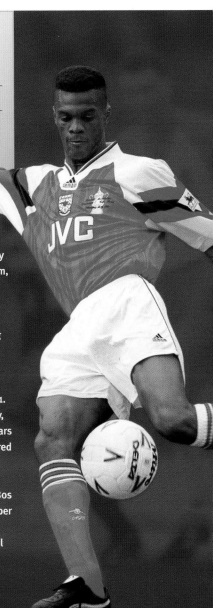

PAUL DAVIS
(1979/80–1994/95)

POSITION:
MIDFIELDER

APPEARANCES:
445

GOALS:
37

BORN:
DULWICH, LONDON,
9 DECEMBER 1961

CLUB HONOURS:
LEAGUE CHAMPIONSHIP 1989,
1991; FA CUP 1993; EUROPEAN
CUP WINNERS' CUP 1994; LEAGUE
CUP 1987, 1993

OTHER CLUBS:
STABAEK, BRENTFORD

Paul Davis is known as being a gentleman, and just as his gentle manners have made him stand out off the field, so did his cultured technique mark him as special on it. His football philosophy was, at times, somewhat at odds with those of George Graham, but he earned enormous affection from everyone associated with the Club.

Making his debut in 1980 against arch-rivals Tottenham Hotspur, Davis became a mainstay of the Arsenal team during the 1980s and was awarded the captaincy when first Kenny Sansom and then Tony Adams were unavailable. With extraordinary vision and a sweet left foot, he played a significant role in the league championships of 1989 and 1991.

After a disagreement with Graham over aspects of his play, Davis made only occasional appearances during the latter years of his Arsenal career. However, his cameos were always cheered by the fans – not least his star role throughout the successful European Cup Winners' Cup run in 1993–94.

Ask any Arsenal fan who watched the team during the 1980s and early 1990s about Davis, and they will, no doubt, remember a diligent and loyal servant. It is no surprise that he has now returned to the Club as a Youth Coach. He has also had a spell as Assistant Manager of Kettering Town.

TONY ADAMS

It is tempting to say that the many honours won by Tony Adams during his Arsenal career tell his story better than words could. However, they only begin to paint the picture of this extraordinary man. A fearless player and captain, his 18 years at Highbury gave him a status that is little short of iconic.

TONY ADAMS
(1983/84–2001/02)

POSITION:
DEFENDER

APPEARANCES:
668

GOALS:
49

BORN:
ROMFORD, ESSEX,
10 OCTOBER 1966

CLUB HONOURS:
LEAGUE CHAMPIONSHIP 1989, 1991, 1998, 2002; FA CUP 1993, 1998, 2002; LEAGUE CUP 1987, 1993; EUROPEAN CUP WINNERS' CUP 1994

OTHER HONOURS:
66 ENGLAND CAPS (5 GOALS)

MANAGERIAL CAREER:
WYCOMBE WANDERERS

Tony Adams made his debut in November 1983, just weeks after he turned 17, but it was with the arrival of George Graham in 1986 that Adams's career truly took off. He was ever-present in Graham's first season, and in addition to being part of the League Cup winning side, he was named PFA Young Player of the Year and received an England call-up. The following year he was crowned captain, the youngest in the Club's history at that point.

Adams was perhaps the most complete centre half in the Club's history. He had aerial dominance, organizational expertize and was a fierce tackler. However, he was also a target for opposition fans and newspaper critics who preferred to concentrate on his occasional mistakes. These jibes motivated him.

Captaining Arsenal to league titles in 1989 and 1991, the Essex man could have considered that he had answered his critics. However, his appetite for success had only been whetted by this achievement. As the teams' attention turned to the cups in the mid-1990s, Adams scored key goals – the winners against Spurs in the 1993 FA Cup Semi-final and Torino in the European Cup Winners' Cup the following year.

The arrival of Arsène Wenger turned the story of Tony Adams from being brilliant to extraordinary. Under the Frenchman, Adams seemed to find a new confidence and his memorable left-footed goals against Spurs and Everton in the following two years had everyone shaking their heads with a mixture of joy and surprise. The second strike capped Adams's return from a test in his personal life and a serious injury. It confirmed a victory that landed the Club the Premiership title, too.

There was time for one more title in 2002, making Tony Adams the first Arsenal player to win league titles in three separate decades. He was also the only Arsenal player to captain two Arsenal sides to the Double. Pat Rice says it all: 'What a leader, what a player, what a man.'

After leaving the Club he had a spell as Manager of Wycombe Wanderers. He then became Assistant Manager at Portsmouth.

'A FEARLESS PLAYER AND CAPTAIN, HIS 18 YEARS AT HIGHBURY GAVE HIM A STATUS THAT IS LITTLE SHORT OF ICONIC'

PAUL MERSON

Merson's spirit, capacity for moments of genius and exuberant character made him a favourite among the Arsenal fans even during periods of frustrating inconsistency and well-publicized personal challenges.

PAUL MERSON (1986/87–1996/97)	CLUB HONOURS: LEAGUE CHAMPIONSHIP 1989, 1991; EUROPEAN CUP WINNERS' CUP 1994; FA CUP 1993; LEAGUE CUP 1993
POSITION: STRIKER	
APPEARANCES: 425	OTHER HONOURS: 21 ENGLAND CAPS (3 GOALS)
GOALS: 99	OTHER CLUBS: BRENTFORD, MIDDLESBROUGH, ASTON VILLA, PORTSMOUTH, WALSALL
BORN: HARLESDEN, LONDON, 20 MARCH 1968	MANAGERIAL CAREER: WALSALL 2004–06

Paul Merson truly arrived on the scene during the title-winning 1988–89 season, adding a PFA Young Player of the Year Award to his championship medal.

He failed to live up to this brilliance the following year – as did the team in general – but both team and player bounced back with spirit to lift the title again in 1991. The campaign that followed was trophyless, but included a joyful, goal-crazy run of which Merson was a key architect.

Typical of Merson's artistry was his opener in the 1993 League Cup Final against Sheffield Wednesday. With the ball loose outside the penalty area, Merson hit it first time sending a dipping shot past the helpless Chris Woods. He was also effective from set-pieces, as when he scored from a long-range free-kick against Standard Liege in the following season's European Cup Winners' Cup tie.

After leaving the fray to deal with his personal problems, Merson returned fitter, leaner and also somewhat more disciplined. That said, his trademark roving runs were still seen regularly and he continued to notch up some wonderful goals. He performed well in Wenger's first season in charge but made the decision to leave in 1997 to secure the regular first team football he craved.

Merson produced some of his finest form of his career with Middlesbrough and was also a popular figure among the Aston Villa faithful following his move to Villa Park. He was then instrumental in Portsmouth's promotion to the Premiership in 2003. After his time at Portsmouth, Merson moved into management with a mixed spell at Walsall, and was a regular pundit for Sky. However, Merson will always have a special place in the hearts of the Arsenal faithful.

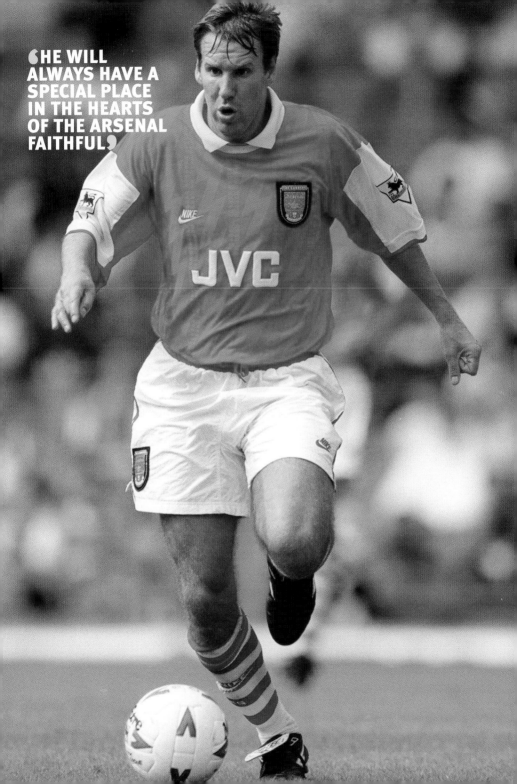

'HE WILL ALWAYS HAVE A SPECIAL PLACE IN THE HEARTS OF THE ARSENAL FAITHFUL'

PERRY GROVES

PERRY GROVES
(1986/87–1992/93)

POSITION:
MIDFIELDER

APPEARANCES:
199

GOALS:
25

BORN:
BOW, LONDON,
19 APRIL 1965

CLUB HONOURS:
LEAGUE CHAMPIONSHIP 1989,
1991; LEAGUE CUP 1987

OTHER CLUBS:
COLCHESTER UNITED,
SOUTHAMPTON

The first signing by George Graham, Perry Groves fully justified the Manager's faith in him when his efforts on the flanks were key factors in Arsenal's 1989 and 1991 league championship victories.

During these times where an unbeaten Premiership season was followed not long after by a Champions League Final it is easy to forget quite how enjoyable and significant the 1987 League Cup Final victory was for Arsenal. For that glorious afternoon, we have Perry Groves to thank as much as anyone – for it was he that set up Charlie Nicholas's winner.

Many of his appearances during the memorable campaigns of 1989 and 1991 came as a substitute – and often a very effective one at that. He was full of enthusiasm and spirit and on occasion would make opposition defenders look ordinary.

After the 1991 championship, so much seemed to change at Arsenal. The tactics became more cautious and a number of personnel changes were made in subsequent years. One of those was the sale of Groves to Southampton where a serious Achilles tendon injury forced him to retire at the age of 28.

JOHN LUKIC

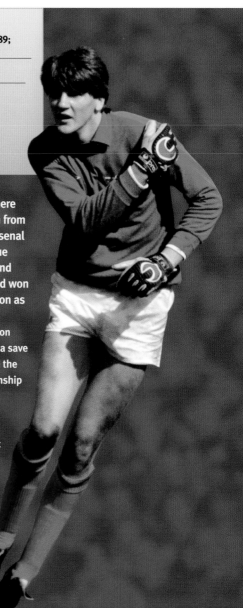

JOHN LUKIC
(1983/84–1989/90 &
1996/7–2000/01)

POSITION:
GOALKEEPER

APPEARANCES:
293

BORN:
CHESTERFIELD,
DERBYSHIRE,
11 DECEMBER 1960

CLUB HONOURS:
LEAGUE CHAMPIONSHIP 1989;
LEAGUE CUP 1987

OTHER CLUBS:
LEEDS UNITED

John Lukic started his career at Leeds United, where his great form prevented a young David Seaman from getting a place in the side. Lukic then moved to Arsenal where he succeeded Pat Jennings and won a league championship before being replaced by Seaman and leaving the Club. He went back to Leeds United and won a league title there before returning to North London as Seaman's number two.

Arriving at Arsenal aged 22, he quickly drew attention with his exceptional shot-stops and the way he turned a save into an attack so crisply. Most memorably, he launched the attack which led to Michael Thomas's league-championship clinching goal at Anfield in 1989.

It is a mark of Lukic's popularity that when David Seaman replaced him, it took the Yorkshireman some time to win over the fans who had mourned when Lukic left the Club. For his part, Lukic bounced back quickly at Elland Road.

In 1996, he returned to Highbury where he proved an able and popular deputy for Seaman. He remained on the playing staff until he turned 40 when he retired. Since then he has been involved with coaching goalkeepers.

MARTIN KEOWN

Martin Keown began his Arsenal career in the mid-1980s as a teenage centre-back with hopes of becoming the defensive partner of David O'Leary.

MARTIN KEOWN (1985/86 & 1992/93–2003/04)	BORN: OXFORD, OXFORDSHIRE, 24 JULY 1966
POSITION: DEFENDER	CLUB HONOURS: LEAGUE CHAMPIONSHIP 1998, 2002, 2004; FA CUP 1998, 2002, 2003
APPEARANCES: 449	OTHER HONOURS: 43 ENGLAND CAPS (2 GOALS)
GOALS: 8	OTHER CLUBS: BRIGHTON, ASTON VILLA, EVERTON, LEICESTER CITY, READING

However, after just half a season of first-team football, he was sold to Aston Villa. Keown returned six years later in 1992 as a utility man, playing in a number of positions and transformed himself under the reign of Arsène Wenger.

The Oxford man was never the sort of player who was popular among fans of other clubs, but then, neither did he court any such affection. A supremely focused individual, Keown just wanted to win. He was extremely quick and effective in the tackle. He could shadow a player so well he was sometimes also employed as a man-marker, particularly in European ties.

He missed out when both domestic cups were won in 1993 due to being cup-tied. He was also sidelined with injury when the team won the Cup Winners' Cup in 1994. However, this only served to fuel his hunger as Arsenal went on to win the Double in 1998, landing Keown the first two medals of his career in North London.

Perhaps his finest personal hour came in September 2000 when he scored twice in the final five minutes to hand Arsenal victory over Shakhtar Donetsk in the Champions League. His heroics were all the more impressive given that he was carrying a thigh injury at the time.

He won four more medals – two FA Cup and two Premiership – before retiring in 2004 after playing an integral role in the unbeaten season. Keown was a passionate competitor; occasionally his passion was evident in very direct challenges, leading to more disapproval among opposition fans. As for the Arsenal supporters, they adored him and were delighted that this Arsenal man had returned to the fold in 1992.

‘A SUPREMELY FOCUSED INDIVIDUAL, KEOWN JUST WANTED TO WIN’

STEVE BOULD

Arsenal famously managed an unbeaten league season in 2004, but 13 years earlier they came agonisingly close to completing the same illustrious feat.

STEVE BOULD (1988/89–1998/99)	CLUB HONOURS: LEAGUE CHAMPIONSHIP 1989,
POSITION: DEFENDER	1991, 1998; EUROPEAN CUP WINNERS' CUP 1994
APPEARANCES: 372	OTHER HONOURS: 2 ENGLAND CAPS
GOALS: 8	OTHER CLUBS: STOKE CITY, TORQUAY UNITED,
BORN: STOKE-ON-TRENT, STAFFORDSHIRE, 16 NOVEMBER 1962	SUNDERLAND

It is no surprise that the team's sole defeat came in a tie where Steve Bould was forced to leave the field due to injury. Many observers – George Graham included – insist that had Bould been able to remain on the field in that clash with London rivals Chelsea, the unbeaten run would have continued.

It would be wrong to say that Bould was an elegant or extravagant player, he was however enormously powerful and reliable. His no-nonsense, aggressive style made him an instant hit at Highbury when he arrived from Stoke City in 1988. As the good times returned to the Club, Bould was the lynchpin of the Arsenal sides that won the league twice in his first three years in North London.

Injury robbed him of a place in Arsenal's victorious FA Cup and League Cup finals in 1993 but he had made a key contribution in booking the team's trips to the twin towers of the national stadium. Then, in the consequent European Cup Winners' Cup campaign, he made up for his Wembley absence. Never was Bould more impressive than in the Final against Parma in Copenhagen; a key component of the rearguard that put the 'nil' in the fans' chant of 'One-nil to the Arsenal'.

Arsène Wenger's arrival at the Club seemed to liberate Bould, who showed more poise than ever under the Frenchman. When Arsenal secured the Premiership title in 1998, he underlined this change in style. As well as helping shut Everton out on the day the championship was clinched, he dinked a fine ball through to set up his long-term defensive ally Tony Adams to crown the day with a left-footed strike.

Arsenal fans' gratitude for having witnessed such a powerful and able defender will be forever tinged with confusion as to how he never received greater recognition away from the Club, particularly from successive England managers. However, the national team's loss was Arsenal's gain. Bould left the Club in 1999 for Sunderland but has since returned as part of the successful Arsenal Academy.

'HE WAS A KEY COMPONENT OF THE REARGUARD THAT PUT THE 'NIL' IN THE FANS' CHANT OF 'ONE-NIL TO THE ARSENAL'

KEVIN
CAMPBELL

KEVIN CAMPBELL
(1987/88–1994/95)
POSITION:
STRIKER
APPEARANCES:
228
GOALS:
59
BORN:
LAMBETH, LONDON,
4 FEBRUARY 1970

CLUB HONOURS:
LEAGUE CHAMPIONSHIP 1991;
FA CUP 1993; LEAGUE CUP 1993;
EUROPEAN CUP WINNERS' CUP
1994
OTHER CLUBS:
LEYTON ORIENT, LEICESTER CITY,
NOTTINGHAM FOREST,
TRABZONSPOR, EVERTON,
WEST BROM ALBION,
CARDIFF CITY

When he left Arsenal in 1995, Kevin Campbell took with him winners' medals from the League Championship, the FA Cup, League Cup and European Cup Winners' Cup. Despite this bountiful haul, he is still remembered as a player who disappointed – a measure of the high expectations that surrounded him when he emerged from the youth ranks.

Campbell had been incredibly prolific as a youngster, starring at youth level and scoring a remarkable 94 goals in 89 reserve outings. This muscular, explosive striker seemed to have the world at his feet. After some promising first-team outings in the late 1980s, Campbell captured attention when his eight goals in 10 games during the 1990–91 run-in helped the Gunners lift the championship trophy.

For the remainder of his time with Arsenal, Campbell seemed to lose the confidence that had fired him in his younger days. Not that it was all gloom: he took part in the Double-cup triumph in 1993 and was a key member of the side that won the European Cup Winners' Cup the following year.

He moved to Nottingham Forest in 1995. He then moved to Turkey and returned to England with Everton in 1998.

COLIN PATES

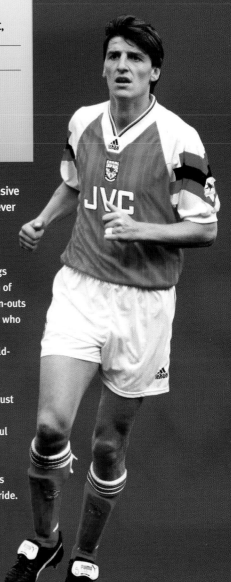

COLIN PATES
(1989/90–1992/93)

POSITION:
DEFENDER

APPEARANCES:
25

GOALS:
1

BORN:
CARSHALTON, LONDON,
10 AUGUST 1961

OTHER CLUBS:
CHELSEA, CHARLTON ATHLETIC,
BRIGHTON

MANAGERIAL CAREER:
CRAWLEY TOWN

Signing for a Club that already boasted the defensive prowess of Tony Adams and Steve Bould was never going to be easy for any defensive player.

Therefore, it is not surprising that Colin Pates made relatively few appearances during his three-and-a-half years with the Club. Not that the sparseness of his outings should detract from the competence and professionalism of the London-born defender. He bided his time between run-outs without complaint and trained with the dedication of one who was playing every week.

When the former Chelsea man was called upon, his old-fashioned, unfussy style of defending was consistently effective. Stamping out any threat almost as soon as it appeared, he had a steadiness about him that inspired trust from the Arsenal faithful.

In 1991, Pates put Arsenal in the lead during the fateful European Cup tie against Benfica. Sadly, it proved to be a false dawn and the team lost on the night. Pates left Arsenal for Brighton, and has since had spells working as a manager. He can look back on his Arsenal years with pride.

Did you hear the one about the two Englishmen, the Dutchman and the Frenchman? Well it was four such men who scored 100 or more goals for Arsenal and whose careers coincided with the Premiership years. They are Alan Smith, Ian Wright, Dennis Bergkamp and Thierry Henry.

THE 100 CLUB!

To score 100 goals for your team is an incredible achievement: only 16 players in the Club's history have scored 100 goals or more. Here is the low-down on the four players who have achieved this during the Premiership years... .

▲ *Clockwise from top: Alan Smith strokes home the winning goal of the 1994 European Cup Winners' Cup Final; Ian Wright celebrates his 179th goal for Arsenal; Dennis Bergkamp and Thierry Henry celebrate another goal (V Everton, 15 August 2004).*

ALAN SMITH

FIRST ARSENAL GOAL:
V PORTSMOUTH, 29 AUGUST 1987, LEAGUE DIVISION ONE (HOME)

100TH GOAL:
V COVENTRY CITY, 7 DECEMBER 1992

STRIKE RATE:
REACHED 100 GOALS IN 251 GAMES

DID YOU KNOW:
WHEN ALAN SMITH SIGNED FOR ARSENAL, FUTURE CENTURION THIERRY HENRY WAS JUST 9 YEARS OLD.

IAN WRIGHT

FIRST ARSENAL GOAL:
V LEICESTER CITY, 25 SEPTEMBER 1991,
LEAGUE CUP (AWAY)

100TH GOAL:
V CRYSTAL PALACE, 1 OCTOBER 1994

STRIKE RATE:
REACHED 100 GOALS IN 143 GAMES

DID YOU KNOW:
IN THE 1992/93 SEASON, WRIGHT SCORED 30 OF
ARSENAL'S 73 GOALS IN ALL TOURNAMENTS –
THAT IS 41 PER CENT OF THE CLUB'S GOALS!

DENNIS BERGKAMP

FIRST ARSENAL GOAL:
V SOUTHAMPTON, 23 SEPTEMBER 1995,
PREMIERSHIP (HOME)

100TH GOAL:
V OXFORD IN JANUARY 2003

STRIKE RATE:
REACHED 100 GOALS IN 296 GAMES

DID YOU KNOW:
DENNIS SCORED JUST ONE HAT-TRICK DURING
HIS ARSENAL CAREER, AGAINST LEICESTER CITY
IN 1997.

THIERRY HENRY

FIRST ARSENAL GOAL:
V SOUTHAMPTON, 18 SEPTEMBER 1999,
PREMIERSHIP (AWAY)

100TH GOAL:
V BIRMINGHAM CITY IN JANUARY 2003

STRIKE RATE:
REACHED 100 GOALS IN 181 GAMES

DID YOU KNOW:
THIERRY HENRY SCORED MORE GOALS IN THE
LEAGUE AND IN EUROPEAN COMPETITION THAN
ANY OTHER STRIKER IN THE CLUB'S HISTORY.

NIGEL WINTERBURN

The gritted teeth and determined expression as both his arms rotate like windmills, whipping up the Highbury faithful: Nigel Winterburn was never one to greet victory quietly.

NIGEL WINTERBURN
(1987/88–1999/2000)

POSITION:
DEFENDER

APPEARANCES:
584

GOALS:
12

BORN:
ARLEY, WARWICKSHIRE, 11 DECEMBER 1963

CLUB HONOURS:
LEAGUE CHAMPIONSHIP 1989, 1991, 1998; FA CUP 1993, 1998; LEAGUE CUP 1993; EUROPEAN CUP WINNERS' CUP 1994

OTHER HONOURS:
2 ENGLAND CAPS

OTHER CLUBS:
WIMBLEDON, WEST HAM UNITED

The left-back had plenty of opportunities to fine-tune his method of celebration – he won a host of trophies with Arsenal including three league championships and a European Cup Winners' Cup.

Winterburn joined Arsenal from Wimbledon and brought with him the finer qualities of that team: determination, courage and a blind refusal to concede defeat. He spent most of his first year at Highbury in the reserves, but in 1988 he broke into the first team, replacing the hugely popular Kenny Sansom. Lesser men would have been intimidated by the prospect of following in the footsteps of a club legend – but not Winterburn.

The key memories that Arsenal fans have of Winterburn are not without irony. He was not a prolific goal-scorer, yet the Gunners faithful will always remember him for two spectacular strikes. Perhaps the more significant strike was his long-range goal against his old team Wimbledon, as Arsenal closed in on the 1989 league championship. The irony is doubled here as he unleashed the volley with his right foot – a foot that some accused him of being unable to kick with. The other strike was his last-gasp shot from 25 yards that won an exciting Derby against Chelsea at Stamford Bridge in September 1997.

Why Winterburn only won two England caps during his highly successful career is a mystery. It is only partially solved by acknowledging that the presence of Stuart Pearce in the international fold coincided with the Arsenal man's career.

Back at club level, Winterburn was written off time after time, and when Arsène Wenger arrived in 1996, many felt that the 33-year-old would be surplus to requirements. However, as with so many of the squad, Winterburn seemed to find a second wind under the Frenchman's tutelage and had plenty more opportunities to perform his windmill celebration before moving to West Ham United in 2000.

'LESSER MEN WOULD HAVE BEEN INTIMIDATED BY THE PROSPECT OF FOLLOWING IN THE FOOTSTEPS OF A CLUB LEGEND – BUT NOT WINTERBURN'

ANDY LINIGHAN

ANDY LINIGHAN
(1990/91–1996/97)

POSITION:
DEFENDER

APPEARANCES:
156

GOALS:
8

BORN:
HARTLEPOOL, COUNTY DURHAM, 18 JUNE 1962

CLUB HONOURS:
LEAGUE CHAMPIONSHIP 1991; FA CUP 1993; LEAGUE CUP 1993

OTHER CLUBS:
HARTLEPOOL UNITED, LEEDS UNITED, OLDHAM ATHLETIC, NORWICH CITY, CRYSTAL PALACE, QUEEN'S PARK RANGERS, OXFORD UNITED

Children across the country dream of scoring the winning goal in an FA Cup Final. Despite his disappointments at Highbury, for Linighan, that dream came true. Star strikers might find the back of the net on a regular basis, but sometimes the magic of the FA Cup can offer up surprise goal scorers who help to write the history of their respective clubs. It is one of the charms of the game of football that Andy Linighan, an old-fashioned centre back who never consistently imposed himself at Highbury, scored just such a goal in the 1993 FA Cup Final.

Linighan arrived in the summer of 1990, along with David Seaman and Anders Limpar. However, he did not influence the subsequent championship-winning campaign in the same way that his fellow new faces did. Thanks to the solid partnership of Adams and Bould, the Hartlepool-born centre back was unable to claim a regular place on the field.

However, he went on to create a key moment in the Club's history. The 1993 FA Cup Final replay was not a classic football encounter but Linighan's last-minute winner will linger long in the memory of all who witnessed it. He played much of the match with a broken nose after a collision with Mark Bright but gloriously out-jumped Bright to head the winner.

DAVID HILLIER

DAVID HILLIER (1990/91–1996/97)	**CLUB HONOURS:** LEAGUE CHAMPIONSHIP 1991
POSITION: MIDFIELDER	**OTHER CLUBS:** PORTSMOUTH, BRISTOL ROVERS, BARNET
APPEARANCES: 143	
GOALS: 2	
BORN: BLACKHEATH, LONDON, 18 DECEMBER 1969	

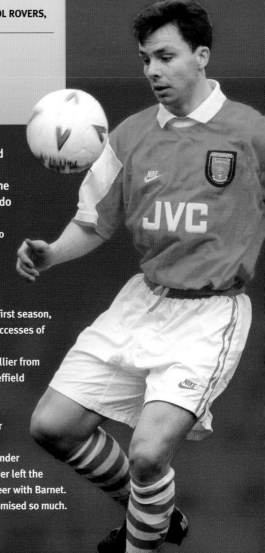

The first half of the 1990s was not a period when the Arsenal midfield was over-subscribed with flair. However, memories of the accurate and incisive passing of David Hillier do emerge to warm the heart.

Hillier had already captained the youth team to the 1988 Youth Cup before he emerged into the first team during the title-winning 1990–91 season. Although an accomplished distributor of the ball, Hillier could also be a fierce tackler. Having won a league championship medal in his first season, the stage seemed set for Hillier to emulate the successes of other home-grown midfielders.

Sadly, a knee injury in April 1993 prevented Hillier from taking part in the Gunners' cup Finals against Sheffield Wednesday. Tragically, it also robbed him of his momentum and meant that the Highbury faithful would be left wondering what could have been for the London-born midfielder.

Although he gave hints of a revival in fortune under Bruce Rioch's eye, it would not be long before Hillier left the Club for Portsmouth, before winding down his career with Barnet. It seemed an unfitting end for a player who had promised so much.

LEE DIXON

In 1984, Burnley released a young winger after he had made just a handful of appearances. Eighteen years later, Lee Dixon retired from football having won eight trophies during his time with Arsenal.

LEE DIXON
(1987/88–2001/02)
POSITION:
DEFENDER
APPEARANCES:
619
GOALS:
27
BORN:
MANCHESTER,
17 MARCH 1964

CLUB HONOURS:
LEAGUE CHAMPIONSHIP 1989,
1991, 1998, 2002; FA CUP 1993,
1998, 2002; EUROPEAN CUP
WINNERS' CUP 1994
OTHER HONOURS:
22 ENGLAND CAPS (1 GOAL)
OTHER CLUBS:
BURNLEY, CHESTER CITY, BURY,
STOKE CITY

Dixon made his name not as a winger, but as a full-back who stopped wingers in their tracks. After leaving Burnley, Dixon played for Chester City, Bury and Stoke City before he was spotted by George Graham and brought to Arsenal in 1988. He quickly became the first choice right-back; his experience as a winger helped him to bomb forward with great effect as Graham demanded.

Dixon's daring raids were a feature of the 1989 and 1991 championship seasons. Time after time, Dixon set up Alan Smith to dispatch another dangerous shot on goal. Not that his forward runs were always offensive; he was always willing to stop an opposition move in its earliest stages. He became an England international, winning 22 caps in total.

Dixon's Arsenal career should not be portrayed as a simple affair. By his own admission, Dixon was not above making mistakes; sometimes quite spectacular ones. Opposition fans would question his credentials

to play for England, but Dixon was far too tough a character to use any setback as anything other than motivation for further success.

Victories continued to come his way as Arsenal followed their 1993 FA Cup win with a glorious sortie into Europe. Throughout the campaigns that saw Arsenal win the Cup Winners' Cup and reach the Final the following year, Dixon excelled, beating many international attackers.

Dixon then found a new lease of life under Arsène Wenger's regime, and his form was so good that he earned a recall to the England team. He collected medals for both legs of the 1998 Double but he admits that it was the second Double in 2002 that really blew him away: 'When we won the Double in 1998 I felt I had done well, but to do it again four years later was the stuff of dreams.' It was a fitting end to the career of an Arsenal servant who made more than 600 appearances for the Club. What a turnaround for the former Burnley winger.

'WHEN WE WON THE DOUBLE IN 1998 I FELT I HAD DONE WELL, BUT TO DO IT AGAIN FOUR YEARS LATER WAS THE STUFF OF DREAMS'

DAVID SEAMAN

No Arsenal fan would dispute that David Seaman is one of the greatest goalkeepers ever to play for the Club. He was the custodian for a golden era in the Club's history and saw off numerous attempts to depose him.

DAVID SEAMAN (1990/91–2002/03)	CLUB HONOURS: LEAGUE CHAMPIONSHIP 1991, 1998, 2002; FA CUP 1993, 1998, 2002, 2003; LEAGUE CUP 1993; EUROPEAN CUP WINNERS CUP 1994
POSITION: GOALKEEPER	
APPEARANCES: 564	
BORN: ROTHERHAM, YORKSHIRE, 19 SEPTEMBER 1963	OTHER HONOURS: 75 ENGLAND CAPS
	OTHER CLUBS: PETERBOROUGH UNITED, BIRMINGHAM CITY, QUEEN'S PARK RANGERS, MANCHESTER CITY

During the 1989–90 season, Arsenal conceded 38 goals and lost 12 games. That summer, David Seaman arrived at the Club. The following season, Arsenal conceded just 18 goals, lost just one game and were crowned league champions. There had been those who had questioned George Graham's judgement in bringing the Yorkshireman to the Club. In just one campaign, Seaman had vindicated the Scot's decision.

So spectacular were his contributions in goal that many of Seaman's saves would be discussed with the same passion that is normally reserved for wonder goals scored by strikers.

Compared favourably with Pat Jennings by goalkeeping coach and former Arsenal keeper Bob Wilson, Seaman was the most complete custodian imaginable. He was superb at shot-stopping and claiming crosses, and he was brave with a lightning-fast response to danger. He was superb at saving penalties too.

After adding FA Cup and League Cup medals to the Championship medal acquired in his first season, some of Seaman's finest performances came in the two subsequent European Cup Winners' Cup campaigns. On the road to the 1994 victory, he kept six clean sheets, including one in the Final, despite carrying a painful rib injury. The following year, his penalty shoot-out heroics against Sampdoria took Arsenal to the Final. There, Nayim intervened to deny a second victory.

His hunger for success was never satisfied and Wenger noted how Seaman trained harder each season, to prevent his advancing years from affecting him. Seaman was in goal as Arsenal won Doubles in 1998 and 2002. One of the Yorkshireman's finest moments came in his final season: a breathtaking save in the 2003 FA Cup semi-final against Sheffield United. After leaving Highbury, Seaman managed only half a season with Manchester City before injury forced him to retire.

'SO SPECTACULAR WERE SEAMAN'S CONTRIBUTIONS THAT MANY OF HIS SAVES WOULD BE DISCUSSED WITH THE SAME PASSION THAT IS NORMALLY RESERVED FOR WONDER GOALS'

ALAN SMITH

'Yeah, I'm quite pleased. It's just a great night for Arsenal Football Club.' Unpretentious and with a team mentality to the fore, these words, with which Alan Smith greeted his winning goal in the 1994 European Cup Winners' Cup Final, reflect the way he served the club.

ALAN SMITH (1987/88–1994/95)	CLUB HONOURS: LEAGUE CHAMPIONSHIP 1989, 1991; FA CUP 1993; EUROPEAN CUP WINNERS' CUP 1994
POSITION: STRIKER	
APPEARANCES: 347	OTHER HONOURS: 13 ENGLAND CAPS (2 GOALS)
GOALS: 115	OTHER CLUBS: LEICESTER CITY
BORN: BROMSGROVE, WORCESTERSHIRE, 21 NOVEMBER 1962	

Smith, who joined the Gunners in 1987, was an old-fashioned target man who was the focal point of the attack for some of the Club's finest years. He was the leading goal-scorer for Arsenal's title triumphs in 1989 and 1991. Thriving on fantastic service from the wing – first from Brian Marwood and then from Anders Limpar – he tormented defences across the country throughout those triumphant seasons and became an England international as a result of his fine club form.

Never one to seek or bask in public acclaim, he nevertheless had a fine habit of shining on the big occasion. He scored in the 1988 League Cup Final, netted the opener at Anfield on that momentus night in 1989 and produced a vital assist for Thomas's last-minute winner. He scored four against Austria Vienna as Arsenal returned to European Cup competition in 1991.

Then there was the sweet strike against Parma in 1994 that left him 'quite pleased'. Lee Dixon sent a left-footed pass towards the area and Lorenzo Minotti's clearance fell straight to Smith who calmly controlled it and drilled a left-footed shot past Bucci into the net. Having been overshadowed by Ian Wright for some time, Smith's big moment came when Wright was suspended.

In truth, the goal was his last significant contribution to Arsenal, and injury forced him to retire the following spring. He was such an unselfish and tireless player, and it is tempting to think that a player who gave so much was always destined to leave the game early.

Despite his straightforward vocabulary after the 1994 European Cup Final, Smith has since become an astute and articulate observer of the game on television and in newspapers.

‘NEVER ONE TO SEEK OR BASK IN PUBLIC ACCLAIM, HE NEVERTHELESS HAD A FINE HABIT OF SHINING ON THE BIG OCCASION’

The Premiership era has been packed full of highs for Arsenal Football Club. From title-winning strikes, to wonder goals and high-scoring thrillers, there has been plenty for the Gunners' faithful to enjoy. Here is a selection of the finest matches and most memorable goals.

HIGH FIVES!

HIGH FIVE MATCHES

ARSENAL 7 EVERTON 0
11 MAY 2005

The day before this match, Dennis Bergkamp turned 36. However, the Dutchman belied his age and was simply sublime during this tie, setting up the first three goals, scoring the sixth, and pulling the strings all night. There was even time for Edu to score a penalty, his last goal at Highbury, in front of the North Bank as the Gunners demolished Everton.

MANCHESTER UNITED 0 ARSENAL 1
8 MAY 2002

The game that settled the 2001–02 title was a tense encounter, with Manchester United not keen to surrender the Premiership crown without a fight. In the 57th minute, Sylvain Wiltord scored the winner when he pounced upon a loose ball after Fabien Barthez had parried a shot from Freddie Ljungberg. Arsenal only needed one point from the encounter to reclaim the Premiership title, but it was typical of their form during a hard-fought campaign that they won all three points.

MANCHESTER UNITED 0 ARSENAL 1
14 MARCH 1998

One could almost feel the balance of power tilting from the North West of England to North London after this magnificent victory. Alex Manninger performed heroically in goal, Emmanuel Petit dominated the midfield, and Marc Overmars slotted home past Peter Schmeichel to win the game. After that goal, Gary Neville held his head in his hands – this victory did not win Arsenal the league, but it foreshadowed what was to come.

ARSENAL 3 TOTTENHAM 1
24 NOVEMBER 1996

This game produced one of the most exciting climaxes ever to a North London derby. With the score locked at 1-1 and rain lashing down over Highbury, Tony Adams controlled the ball calmly with his chest and scored with a sweet left-footed volley. Minutes later, Bergkamp showed similar composure to curl home in a hectic penalty area. The Dutchman celebrated by skidding with joy across the wet turf. Meanwhile, pandemonium also broke out in the stands. This derby was the dawn of the Wenger era.

LIVERPOOL 0 ARSENAL 2
23 AUGUST 1992

After dramatically winning the league title at Anfield in 1989, the Gunners repeated that 2-0 scoreline in this exciting tie. Second-half goals from Ian Wright and Anders Limpar gave the Club its first Premiership victory over Liverpool. A young Ray Parlour came of age during this exciting encounter.

HIGH FIVE GOALS

THIERRY HENRY V MANCHESTER UNITED
ARSENAL 1 MANCHESTER UNITED 0
1 OCTOBER 2000

The Frenchman has scored so many wonderful goals and this – an early strike in his Arsenal career – was arguably the greatest. At the edge of the penalty area he flicked the ball up and then turned to swerve an unstoppable volley into the corner of the net. It was his first goal for seven weeks – what a way to end his mini-drought!

TONY ADAMS V EVERTON
ARSENAL 4 EVERTON 0
3 MAY 1998

With the Gunners already three goals ahead in this title-clinching match, a fourth goal would normally have been mere icing on the cake. However, when a lobbed pass from Steve Bould was volleyed home from the left foot of Tony Adams, Highbury erupted as if the goal had been a match-winner. The celebration from Adams, with his arms outstretched, has become an iconic Arsenal image of triumph. This strike crystallized the transformation of Tony Adams and Arsenal under its magnificent new manager.

DAVID PLATT V MANCHESTER UNITED
ARSENAL 3 MANCHESTER UNITED 2
9 NOVEMBER 1997

Arsenal went 2-0 ahead and sent the home fans into raptures, only for United to peg them back to 2-2. In the closing stages, David Platt rose to nod home a corner and win the game for Arsenal. A goal of immense importance for the destiny of the 1997/98 Premiership.

DENNIS BERGKAMP V LEICESTER CITY
ARSENAL 3 LEICESTER CITY 3
27 AUGUST 1997

The Dutchman scored a hat-trick on this balmy night at Filbert Street, and while all three goals were beauties, the third was his best. He controlled a cross with his left foot, moved the ball to his right foot and knocked it past the on-rushing home keeper.

IAN WRIGHT V EVERTON
ARSENAL 2 EVERTON 0
28 AUGUST 1993

Many would use the word 'magic' to describe the genius of Wright's goal-scoring ability. However, for this goal he was more of a juggler than a magician. Wright juggled the ball from knee to knee to outfox his marker and then lobbed the ball over Neville Southall.

RAY PARLOUR

Under George Graham's reign, Ray Parlour won a clutch of medals including one in European competition. Despite enjoying such success, the industrious midfielder was not one to rest on his laurels.

RAY PARLOUR
(1991/92 – 2003/04)
POSITION:
MIDFIELDER
APPEARANCES:
467
GOALS:
32
BORN:
ROMFORD, ESSEX, 7 MARCH 1973

CLUB HONOURS:
LEAGUE CHAMPIONSHIP 1998, 2002, 2004; FA CUP 1998, 2002, 2003; LEAGUE CUP 1993; EUROPEAN CUP WINNERS' CUP 1994
OTHER HONOURS:
10 ENGLAND CAPS
OTHER CLUBS:
MIDDLESBROUGH, HULL CITY

When Arsène Wenger arrived he transformed the Essex man's career, and helped him achieve even greater heights.

The early 1990s had few halcyon days when it came to the Arsenal midfield. In Parlour's third game for the Club he starred in a 2-0 win at Anfield, but in general, he rarely stood out above the other midfield hustlers on the Club's books. Bruce Rioch moved Parlour from the right of midfield into the centre and this seemed to freshen him up – but the best was yet to come.

More than any other Arsenal player, Parlour found a new lease of life under Wenger's eye. His game became more creative and far more effective. His Man of the Match award for the 1998 FA Cup Final win over Newcastle United was just one highlight of his contribution to that season's Double. As the Gunners repeated the feat in 2002, Parlour was again influential,

opening the scoring with a smashing strike as Arsenal beat Chelsea in the FA Cup Final.

It was only right that Parlour should have grabbed a star-billing in such a vital game because it was his hard work that had underpinned the Club's glorious campaign. The high esteem he was held in by his team-mates was clear to see in the exuberant celebrations that followed the final whistle.

Parlour left Arsenal for Middlesbrough in 2004 and many Arsenal fans admitted that it was only once his move was confirmed that they realized just how much affection they had held for the man jokingly nicknamed 'Romford Pele' by Marc Overmars. He has been an effective performer in the red shirt of Middlesbrough, but his most profitable days to date have definitely come in the red shirt of Arsenal, and it is his days in North London that most football fans remember him for.

'MORE THAN ANYONE, PARLOUR FOUND A NEW LEASE OF LIFE UNDER WENGER. HIS GAME BECAME CRISPER, MORE CREATIVE AND FAR MORE EFFECTIVE'

STEVE
MORROW

STEVE MORROW
(1991/92–1996/97)
POSITION:
DEFENDER
APPEARANCES:
85
GOALS:
3
BORN:
BELFAST, IRELAND,
2 JULY 1970

CLUB HONOURS:
LEAGUE CUP 1993; EUROPEAN CUP
WINNERS' CUP 1994
OTHER HONOURS:
39 NORTHERN IRELAND CAPS
OTHER CLUBS:
WATFORD, READING, BARNET,
QUEEN'S PARK RANGERS,
PETERBOROUGH UNITED,
DALLAS BURN

Steve Morrow may have only scored three goals for Arsenal, but one of them was a winner in a Wembley Final. And while making just 85 appearances for the Club, one of these included a victorious European Final. However, despite having had some fantastic moments in an Arsenal shirt, he will always be remembered for a bizarre accident. Having scored the winning goal against Sheffield Wednesday in the 1993 League Cup Final, Morrow's day of joy turned to agony when captain Tony Adams dropped the Ulsterman, who broke his arm as he landed on the hallowed turf. He was stretchered from the pitch, breathing through an oxygen mask.

This did not just curtail Morrow's celebrations on the day, it also brought to an end some fine form from the utility man. Having been forced to bide his time before getting first-team action, Morrow had performed with competence in a number of positions.

His finest hour came the following season when he played in place of the injured John Jensen in the European Cup Winners' Cup Final victory over Parma. Morrow's post-Arsenal career has seen him enjoy spells at Queens Park Rangers and Peterborough United. He has since moved to the USA and has coached in Major League Soccer.

JOHN JENSEN

JOHN JENSEN (1992/93–1995/96)	CLUB HONOURS: **EUROPEAN CUP WINNERS' CUP FINAL 1994; FA CUP 1993**
POSITION: **MIDFIELDER**	OTHER HONOURS: **69 DENMARK CAPS (4 GOALS)**
APPEARANCES: **138**	OTHER CLUBS: **BRONDBY, HAMBURG, HERFOLGE BK**
GOALS: **1**	
BORN: **COPENHAGEN, DENMARK, 3 MAY 1965**	

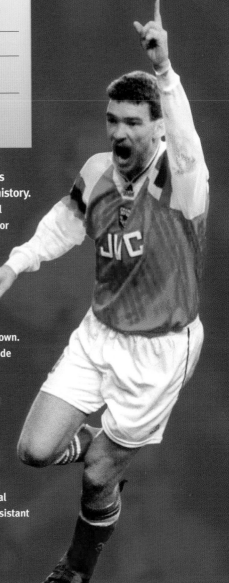

E very Arsenal fan wants to be able to boast: 'I was there' during significant moments in the Club's history. How lucky are those who can boast that they saw Michael Thomas win the league championship at Anfield in 1989, or Tony Adams lift the European Cup Winners' Cup in 1994?

Or those who saw John Jensen score a consolation goal during a 3-1 defeat by Queens Park Rangers on New Year's Eve 1994. Such had become the soap opera regarding the Dane's failure to score in his first two seasons at Arsenal, his beautiful goal that afternoon almost brought the house down.

Jensen was a far more able performer than many outside Highbury gave him credit for. An extremely honest, hard-working midfielder, he was content to concentrate on the simple tasks: win the ball and pass it on. The respect and admiration his team-mates felt for him was clear.

The tragedy of Jensen's Arsenal years is that injury denied him a place in the European Cup Winners' Cup Final of 1994 in his hometown. However, he was still awarded a medal for his efforts in getting the Club to the Final. It was the least he deserved to take from his Arsenal career. The Dane has since had spells as manager and assistant manager with two Danish clubs.

ANDERS LIMPAR

Often in football, the views of a club's supporters and those of the manager are in strict tandem as to the worthiness of a player. Often, but not always as the case of this Swedish winger amply proves.

ANDERS LIMPAR (1990/91–1993/94)	CLUB HONOURS: LEAGUE CHAMPIONSHIP 1991
POSITION: MIDFIELDER	OTHER HONOURS: 58 SWEDEN CAPS (6 GOALS)
APPEARANCES: 116	OTHER CLUBS: BROMMÅPOJKARNA, ORGRYTE, YOUNG BOYS, CREMONESE, EVERTON, BIRMINGHAM CITY, SOLNA, COLORADO RAPIDS, DJURGARDENS IF
GOALS: 20	
BORN: SOLNA, SWEDEN, 24 SEPTEMBER 1965	

Anders Limpar was a player who more than most caused the Arsenal faithful to be at odds with manager George Graham. The fans saw a daring, entertaining winger; the manager saw an increasingly erratic and therefore dangerous luxury.

When he arrived from Cremonese in 1990, the 'Super Swede' quickly added much needed attacking flair to the Arsenal team. A classic winger, he regularly had the crowd in raptures as he bombed forward, humiliating anyone who tried to stop him. He was adept at both setting up goals – as he did to memorable effect for all four of Ian Wright's goals against Everton in December 1991 – and scoring himself.

Just as Brian Marwood had dove-tailed perfectly with Alan Smith during the 1988–89 League Championship winning campaign, so did Limpar provide much of Smith's ammunition when the title was reclaimed in 1991. All seemed to be going well for the Swede. However, following his first excellent season with the Club, Limpar's form became more erratic, producing an increasingly tense relationship with George Graham. Graham had never been one to indulge luxury players, nor fear confrontations with popular team members if he felt such actions were important for the team. Their disagreements over how many international matches Limpar should be allowed to take part in did nothing to help the atmosphere between player and manager.

Limpar had long since dropped out of regular first-team placing by the time he was sold to Everton in 1993. However, Limpar would always remain popular to the Arsenal faithful as they remembered the darting runs, the crucial strikes and the lob from the halfway line during the victory over Liverpool in 1992. He now runs a bar in Sweden: cheers Anders!

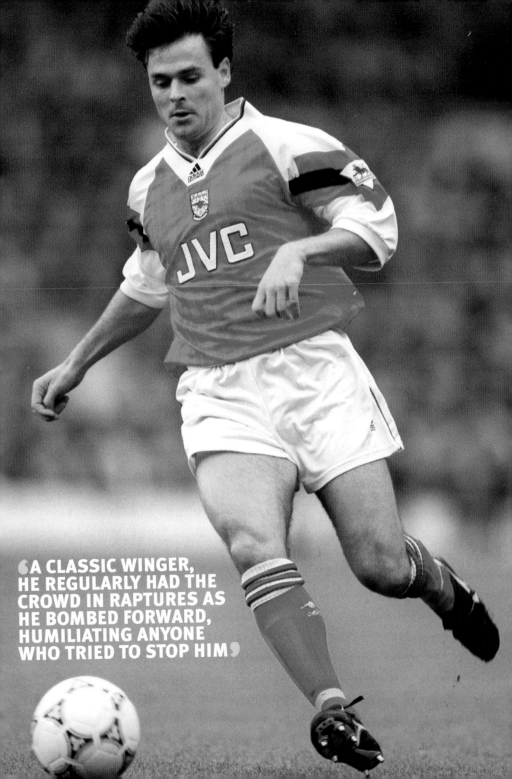

‘A CLASSIC WINGER, HE REGULARLY HAD THE CROWD IN RAPTURES AS HE BOMBED FORWARD, HUMILIATING ANYONE WHO TRIED TO STOP HIM’

NEIL HEANEY

JIMMY CARTER

NEIL HEANE
(1991/92–1993/94)

POSITION:
MIDFIELDER

APPEARANCES:
7

BORN:
MIDDLESBROUGH,
CLEVELAND,
3 NOVEMBER 1971

OTHER CLUBS:
HARTLEPOOL UNITED,
CAMBRIDGE UNITED,
SOUTHAMPTON,
MANCHESTER CITY,
CHARLTON ATHLETIC,
BRISTOL CITY,
DARLINGTON, DUNDEE
UNITED, PLYMOUTH
ARGYLE

JIMMY CARTER
(1991/92–1994/95)

POSITION:
MIDFIELDER

APPEARANCE:
29

GOALS:
2

BORN:
HAMMERSMITH,
LONDON,
9 NOVEMBER 1965

OTHER CLUBS:
CRYSTAL PALACE,
QUEEN'S PARK
RANGERS,
MILLWALL,
LIVERPOOL,
OXFORD UNITED,
PORTSMOUTH,
ODENSE

A two-footed, intelligent winger with the strength to withstand biting challenges and a decent shot in him; Neil Heaney should have done better out of football. However, just as the FA Youth Cup-winner failed to impose himself into an Arsenal first team crying out for some talent on the flanks, so did he struggle to settle anywhere else.

Jimmy Carter made just six appearances during his first season with the Gunners and fared little better in subsequent campaigns. Fast, and with great control, Carter was indisputably blessed with much good skill. His finest hour for the Club came when he scored twice in a tie against Southampton in March 1993.

PAL LYDERSEN

ALAN MILLER

PAL LYDERSEN
(1991/92–1992/93)
POSITION:
DEFENDER
APPEARANCES:
16
BORN:
KRISTIANSAND,
NORWAY,
10 SEPTEMBER 1965

OTHER HONOURS:
20 NORWEGIAN CAPS
(1 GOAL)
OTHER CLUBS:
IK START,
STURM GRAZ,
MOLDE

ALAN MILLER
(1992/93–1993/94)
POSITION:
GOALKEEPER
APPEARANCES:
8
BORN:
EPPING, ESSEX,
29 MARCH 1970

OTHER CLUBS:
PLYMOUTH ARGYLE,
WEST BROMWICH
ALBION,
BIRMINGHAM,
MIDDLESBROUGH,
GRIMSBY,
BLACKBURN ROVERS,
BRISTOL CITY,
COVENTRY CITY,
ST JOHNSTONE

Few in England had heard of Lydersen when he arrived in the autumn of 1991. He could defend and distribute with a capability which could rarely be doubted. Lydersen eventually returned to his homeland, rather than wait for Dixon or Winterburn to be dropped. The Norwegian has since had spells as manager and assistant manager with two Danish clubs.

A lively and enthusiastic goalkeeper, Miller's forte was shot-stopping. A graduate of the FA School of Excellence, with four Under-21 caps, he had few chances to stand-in for David Seaman but he rarely disappointed when given the nod. In 1994, Miller moved to Middlesbrough, collecting a First Division championship medal in his first season.

IAN
WRIGHT

'And it's Ian Wright, Ian Wright FC...' So sang the Arsenal faithful on occasion during the 1992–93 season; a song that reflected Ian Wright's goal-scoring feats and deep bond with the supporters.

IAN WRIGHT	CLUB HONOURS:
(1991/92–1997/98)	LEAGUE CHAMPIONSHIP 1998;
POSITION:	FA CUP 1993; LEAGUE CUP 1993
STRIKER	OTHER HONOURS:
APPEARANCES:	33 ENGLAND CAPS (9 GOALS)
288	OTHER CLUBS:
GOALS:	CRYSTAL PALACE, WEST HAM
185	UNITED, NOTTINGHAM FOREST,
BORN:	CELTIC, BURNLEY
WOOLWICH, LONDON,	
3 NOVEMBER 1963	

The speed and ease with which Wright acquired legend status may have been surprising for some, as many doubted whether the Crystal Palace striker was a wise transfer target for George Graham. Alan Smith, Paul Merson and Kevin Campbell were firing on all cylinders. Andy Cole was emerging in the wings. Why would Graham, renowned more for his love of defenders than attackers, splash out on Wright?

It was often said that 'George knows', and his knowledge here was spot-on. Wright was a goal-scoring phenomenon at Arsenal. This effervescent character could outpace most defenders and those he could not he would instead outwit with his devilishly quick mind. Many of his 185 goals for the Club were 'wonder goals', but he could score the simple goals too, and was good in the air.

Wright scored a goal on his debut against Leicester City and then achieved a hat-trick in his second Gunners game against Southampton. On the final day of his first season, a hat-trick against Southampton won him the Golden Boot. It was a great start, and set a scoring rate that he rarely strayed from throughout his Arsenal career.

He became the fastest Arsenal player to reach 100 goals for the Club, overturning a record held by Ted Drake for 40 years. Wright then smashed Cliff Bastin's goal-scoring record with his hat-trick against Bolton on 13 September 1997. If you score so many goals, you are going to collect some medals: Wright won a league championship, FA Cup and League Cup with Arsenal.

Although injuries cast a shadow over his final season with the Club, Wright's goals in the opening half of the campaign proved crucial when the Premiership title was lifted in May. He then moved to West Ham United and on to Nottingham Forest, Celtic and Burnley. His legacy lives on at Arsenal: quite literally, in the shape of Thierry Henry who graciously credits Wright's example for some of his success. Imagine if they had played together?

'THIS EFFERVESCENT CHARACTER COULD OUTPACE MOST DEFENDERS AND THOSE HE COULD NOT HE WOULD INSTEAD OUTWIT WITH HIS DEVILISHLY QUICK MIND'

PERFECT PARTNERSHIPS

If you want your team to score plenty of goals, developing or buying top-class strikers is only half the battle. You also need to put together a strike partnership that works. Here are the five greatest Arsenal strike partnerships of the Premiership era to date:

IAN WRIGHT AND KEVIN CAMPBELL (1991–95)

Kevin Campbell's muscular build made him a fantastic foil for Ian Wright's pace and eye for goal. A tireless and selfless worker, Campbell could hold the ball up and muscle opponents out of the game allowing the magnificent Wright to score time and time again. Not that Campbell was shy in front of goal either – he scored plenty of goals including two of the four hat-tricks the pair notched up together during their magnificent 1993–94 season.

▲ Ian Wright and Kevin Campbell (1991–95)

Kevin Campbell says, 'Things just seemed to gel. I read Ian's runs and he read my flicks, but Ian was more of an instinctive striker than me. He was the best in the business'.

IAN WRIGHT AND DENNIS BERGKAMP (1995–98)

The saying 'opposites attract' also seems to apply in front of goal. Outgoing, loud and bubbly, Wright's personality was the opposite of Bergkamp's, but on the field they clicked. Bergkamp's incisive passes unlocked defences and Wright's pace and finishing would do the rest. Wright was most dangerous in the penalty box and Bergkamp preferred to conduct business from further out.

Dennis Bergkamp says, 'When I first joined, it was perfect for me to play with Ian Wright as he knew everything about English goal-scoring and he taught me some lessons. You have to respect the partner, be willing to learn something from him even if there is a ten-year gap in age'.

NICOLAS ANELKA AND DENNIS BERGKAMP (1997–99)

With the young Frenchman as his partner, Bergkamp could drop even deeper because he knew that Anelka's pace could catch any probing pass he unleashed. The Dutchman was full of enthusiasm for the partnership. Anelka was just as delighted with the arrangement as Bergkamp allowed him regularly to run one-on-one with the goalkeeper.

Dennis Bergkamp says, 'The way Nicolas played suited me perfectly because he was always looking to run towards goal. That made it easy for me to predict what he wanted and to know instinctively where he would be on the pitch'.

THIERRY HENRY AND DENNIS BERGKAMP (1999–2006)

Many of the strengths of the Anelka/Bergkamp partnership applied to Bergkamp's duo with Henry. Again, the combination of a Frenchman's pace and the Dutchman's vision paid dividends. However, let us remember that Henry too is a master creator and that he was the architect of many Bergkamp goals.

Thierry Henry says, 'Dennis loved to kill a defence with a pass. He was an absolute dream to play with and we complemented each other well, I feel'.

▲ Dennis Bergkamp and Thierry Henry (1999–2006)

THIERRY HENRY AND ROBIN VAN PERSIE (2004–2007)

Of the five main strike partnerships of Arsenal's Premiership years to date, this is probably the one where the two members had the most in common. Like Henry, van Persie is very fast and loves to score. The Dutchman has also spent time earlier in his career playing as a winger, just like Henry. Both also enjoy creating as much as scoring, making them a terrifying prospect for any defender.

Thierry Henry says, 'He loves to play football, so do I. He likes to try stuff, so do I. When two people are of the same vision you can produce good football. One thing I like about him is that he wants to go and score'.

◀ Thierry Henry and Robin van Persie (2004–2007)

GAVIN
MCGOWAN

MARK
FLATTS

GAVIN MCGOWAN
(1992/93–1997/98)

POSITION:
DEFENDER

APPEARANCES:
7

BORN:
BLACKHEATH,
LONDON,
16 JANUARY 1976

OTHER CLUBS:
LUTON TOWN

MARK FLATTS
(1992/93–1994/95)

POSITION:
MIDFIELDER

APPEARANCES:
18

BORN:
HARINGEY, LONDON,
14 OCTOBER 1972

OTHER CLUBS:
CAMBRIDGE UNITED,
BRIGHTON, BRISTOL
CITY, GRIMSBY TOWN,
TORINO, BARNET,
COLCHESTER UNITED

A member of the 1994 FA Youth Cup-winning team, McGowan was a combative defender who could also play as a defensive midfielder. However, with the Gunners well-stocked in both departments in the mid-1990s, McGowan had to look elsewhere for regular first team football.

When Mark Flatts deputized for crowd favourite Anders Limpar, he managed to have fans off their seats with excitement. The local boy could, on a good day, humiliate a full back. However, occasionally he seemed to suffer from nerves. He spent time with Italian side Torino and a number of English clubs including Barnet and Colchester United.

VINCE BARTRAM

IAN SELLEY

VINCE BARTRAM
(1994/95–1996/97)

POSITION:
GOALKEEPER

APPEARANCES:
12

BORN:
BIRMINGHAM,
7 AUGUST 1968

OTHER CLUBS:
WOLVERHAMPTON
WANDERERS,
BLACKPOOL,
BOURNEMOUTH,
HUDDERSFIELD
TOWN, GILLINGHAM

IAN SELLEY
(1992/93–1996/97)

POSITION:
MIDFIELDER

APPEARANCES:
60

GOALS:
2

BORN:
CHERTSEY, SURREY,
14 JUNE, 1974

CLUB HONOURS:
EUROPEAN CUP
WINNERS' CUP 1994

OTHER CLUBS:
SOUTHEND UNITED,
FULHAM, WIMBLEDON

A springy and agile performer, Bartram replaced Alan Miller as the Club's number two goalkeeper in August 1994. In November of that year, he was thrown into first-team action after David Seaman was injured. His best performances came against Aston Villa and Ipswich Town; he kept a clean sheet on both occasions.

Assured and effective as a tackler and a tireless runner, Ian Selley became a favourite of the crowd whenever he got a run-out. His contribution to the 1994 European Cup Winners' Cup run was outstanding. Then, one February afternoon in 1995, he broke his leg and never regained his previous form either at or away from Arsenal.

PAUL DICKOV

SCOTT MARSHALL

PAUL DICKOV
(1992/93–1996/97)

POSITION:
STRIKER

APPEARANCES:
25

GOALS:
6

BORN:
GLASGOW, SCOTLAND,
1 NOVEMBER 1972

HONOURS:
10 SCOTLAND CAPS
(1 GOAL)

OTHER CLUBS:
LUTON TOWN,
BRIGHTON,
MANCHESTER CITY,
LEICESTER CITY,
BLACKBURN ROVERS

SCOTT MARSHALL
(1992/93–1997/98)

POSITION:
DEFENDER

APPEARANCES:
26

GOALS:
1

BORN:
EDINBURGH,
SCOTLAND,
1 MAY 1973

OTHER CLUBS:
ROTHERHAM UNITED,
SHEFFIELD UNITED,
SOUTHAMPTON,
CELTIC, BRENTFORD,
WYCOMBE
WANDERERS

Standing at just 5ft 6in, what Paul Dickov lacks in height he makes up in enthusiasm and determination. He showed plenty of promise during his Arsenal career, scoring memorable goals against Tottenham Hotspur and Sheffield Wednesday. He left in search of regular first-team action and has been a crowd favourite at his subsequent clubs.

With an effective balance of defensive grit and distributional ability, Marshall was once tipped as 'the next Tony Adams'. His only goal was a smashing header against Newcastle United. However, with so many accomplished defenders ahead of him at the Club, a parting of the ways seemed likely. He joined Southampton in 1998.

EDDIE McGOLDRICK

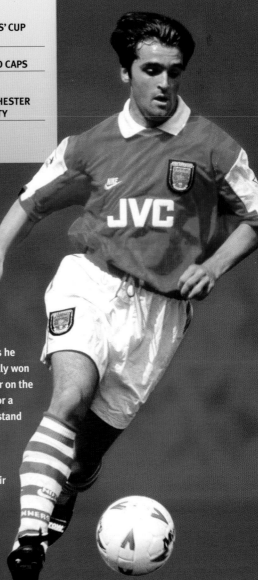

EDDIE McGOLDRICK
(1993/94–1995/96)

POSITION:
MIDFIELDER

APPEARANCES:
57

GOALS:
1

BORN:
ISLINGTON, LONDON,
30 APRIL 1965

CLUB HONOURS:
EUROPEAN CUP WINNERS' CUP
1994

OTHER HONOURS:
20 REPUBLIC OF IRELAND CAPS

OTHER CLUBS:
NORTHAMPTON TOWN,
CRYSTAL PALACE, MANCHESTER
CITY, STOCKPORT COUNTY

I t is safe to say that Eddie McGoldrick had a
fair amount to prove when he signed for
Arsenal in the summer of 1993. He had just
been relegated with Crystal Palace,
missing a gilt-edged chance during
the Eagles' fatal visit to Highbury in
May. Gunners fans had hoped for a
bigger-name signing during the
summer and so the Irishman started
at a disadvantage.

McGoldrick proved to have a strong mentality as he
shrugged off the doubts surrounding him and quickly won
a regular spot in the team. He was a solid performer on the
right flank, making him a very suitable wide-man for a
George Graham team. Add to the mix his ability to stand
in a full-back or sweeper position and you have the
makings of a very useful team member.

However, the lack of flair in his game prevented
the fans from warming to 'Steady Eddie' and it is fair
to say that he enjoyed a less than passionate
relationship with the Arsenal faithful. His best
moment in an Arsenal shirt came with his
spectacular goal against Standard Liege.

STEFAN SCHWARZ

STEFAN SCHWARZ
(1994/95)

POSITION:
MIDFIELDER

APPEARANCES:
49

GOALS:
4

BORN:
MALMO, SWEDEN,
18 APRIL 1969

HONOURS:
69 SWEDEN CAPS

OTHER CLUBS:
MALMO, BENFICA, FIORENTINA,
VALENCIA, SUNDERLAND

We can only speculate on what might have been had Stefan Schwarz remained with Arsenal to play a part of the changes brought in by Bruce Rioch and, then, Arsène Wenger. Instead, Gunners fans were only treated to Stefan Schwarz's astute and industrious displays for just one season.

When he arrived from Benfica in 1994, he brought hope to supporters for whom Arsenal had been short of class in the centre of midfield for too long. He had been a hit in the Portuguese league with Benfica and was fresh from the World Cup Finals where Sweden had finished third.

His delicate features belied a tough customer who seemed perfectly suited to the, at times, brutal bustle of Premiership midfield. A hard worker and a fast mover, it was easy to see why Schwarz had tempted Graham.

However, he left the Club at the end of his first season and moved to Fiorentina. He returned to English football four years later with Sunderland.

JOHN HARTSON

JOHN HARTSON	OTHER HONOURS:
(1994/95–1996/97)	50 WALES CAPS
POSITION:	(14 GOALS)
STRIKER	
APPEARANCES:	OTHER CLUBS:
71	LUTON TOWN,
GOALS:	WEST HAM UNITED,
17	WIMBLEDON,
BORN:	COVENTRY CITY,
SWANSEA, GLAMORGAN,	CELTIC, WEST
5 APRIL 1975	BROMWICH ALBION

When he scored Arsenal's equalizer during the 1995 European Cup Winners' Cup Final in the Parc de Princes against Real Zaragoza, John Hartson did not immediately receive any credit.

The scrambled nature of the finish meant that many initially thought Ian Wright had applied the final touch and therefore chanted Wright's name during the celebrations. This moment is symbolic of how the Welshman was somewhat overshadowed during his Highbury years.

When George Graham signed him in 1995, Hartson became the most expensive British teenage footballer. Although he was tall and powerfully-built he was a very neat player on the ball and was bursting with confidence and ambition. Also adept at holding the ball up, he was as close as Arsenal have come to fielding a 'new Alan Smith' since he retired.

Although Hartson arrived during the turbulent final months of George Graham's reign, he seemed unfazed by the problems the Club was facing. He played with the air of a man who felt he was destined to play on such a high stage.

He moved to West Ham United where he was a huge hit with the fans. He has since played for a number of clubs including a successful and trophy-laden spell at Celtic.

CHRIS KIWOMYA

CHRIS KIWOMYA
(1994/95–1997/98)

POSITION:
STRIKER

APPEARANCES:
17

GOALS:
3

BORN:
**HUDDERSFIELD, YORKSHIRE,
2 DECEMBER 1969**

OTHER CLUBS:
**IPSWICH TOWN, LE HAVRE,
SELANGOR, QUEEN'S PARK
RANGERS, AALBORG**

Kiwomya's career at Arsenal was short and frustrating. However, if it were not for the three goals that he scored during his 17 matches, the history of the Club might have been very different.

One of the final purchases made by George Graham as his reign at the Club reached its bitter conclusion, Kiwomya arrived when the Club was perilously close to the relegation zone. This was unfamiliar territory for Arsenal, but perhaps Kiwomya's experience of it with Ipswich Town helped him face the pressure.

His cool, chipped goal against Nottingham Forest in the first match after George Graham's departure secured three vital points for the team. Together with his two-goal contribution to the victory against Crystal Palace the same week, Kiwomya played a key role in lifting the Gunners onto safer ground.

Once Ian Wright was available again for first-team action, Kiwomya had to wait for occasional opportunities to return to the first team. Bruce Rioch became Arsenal manager that summer, and he did not pick Kiwomya at all for the following campaign. Kiwomya and Arsenal parted company in May 1998.

GLENN ⁵⁵
HELDER

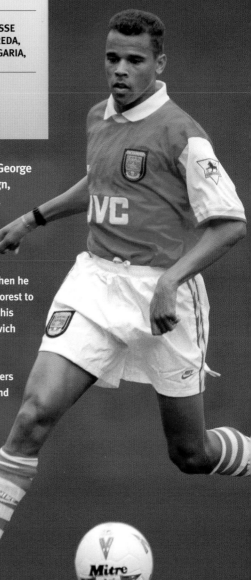

GLENN HELDER
(1994/95–1996/97)

POSITION:
MIDFIELDER

APPEARANCES:
49

GOALS:
1

BORN:
LEIDEN, HOLLAND,
28 OCTOBER 1968

OTHER HONOURS:
4 HOLLAND CAPS

OTHER CLUBS:
SPARTA ROTTERDAM, VITESSE
ARNHEM, BENFICA, NAC BREDA,
DALIAN WANDA, MTK HUNGARIA,
RBC ROOSENDAAL

Glenn Helder was the final signing made by George Graham, yet he never played during his reign, only making his debut after Graham left the Club. This fact is typical of the Dutchman's short Highbury career which was always a little out of kilter.

There was no doubting the ability of Helder, who arrived from Vitesse Arnhem in February 1995. When he stepped off the Highbury bench against Nottingham Forest to make his debut, he mesmerized the home crowd with his pace and trickery. In subsequent outings against Norwich and Ipswich, Helder continued to entertain.

Then Bruce Rioch arrived and brought Dennis Bergkamp to the Club. Bergkamp had thrived off wingers throughout his career, so the idea of combining him and Helder was promising. However, Helder proved infuriatingly inconsistent that season, and became known less for flair and more for some wasteful finishing in front of goal.

After leaving Arsenal, he moved between several clubs. He returned to North London with a cameo appearance in an Arsenal shirt at Dennis Bergkamp's testimonial.

STEPHEN HUGHES

STEPHEN HUGHES
(1994/95–1999/2000)

POSITION:
MIDFIELDER

APPEARANCES:
77

GOALS:
7

BORN:
WOKINGHAM, SURREY,
18 SEPTEMBER 1976

CLUB HONOURS:
LEAGUE CHAMPIONSHIP 1998

OTHER CLUBS:
FULHAM (LOAN), EVERTON,
WATFORD, CHARLTON ATHLETIC,
COVENTRY CITY

Stephen Hughes's Arsenal career may not have lived up to its early promise but the young midfielder was never short of goodwill from the Club's supporters.

Having starred as Arsenal's youngsters marched to FA Youth Cup glory in 1994, Hughes was a name that many Gunners fans were already familiar with before he made his first-team debut the following season. His confident and offensive game suggested a bright future.

In Wenger's first full season, Hughes signed a five-year contract with Arsenal, but his progress seemed to stop at the same time. The likes of Patrick Vieira, Marc Overmars and Emmanuel Petit formed a formidable barrier to the first team, and the energetic and ambitious Hughes grew ever more frustrated.

He became determined to move and after a loan spell with Fulham he signed for Everton. He has since suffered terrible injuries that have stunted his progress.

PAUL
SHAW

ADRIAN
CLARKE

PAUL SHAW
(1994/95–1996/97)
POSITION:
STRIKER
APPEARANCES:
13
GOALS:
2
BORN:
BURNHAM,
BUCKINGHAMSHIRE,
4 SEPTEMBER, 1973

OTHER CLUBS:
BURNLEY, CARDIFF
CITY, PETERBOROUGH
UNITED, MILLWALL,
GILLINGHAM,
SHEFFIELD UNITED,
ROTHERHAM UNITED,
CHESTERFIELD

ADRIAN CLARKE
(1994/95–1995/96)
POSITION:
MIDFIELDER
APPEARANCES:
9
BORN:
CAMBRIDGE,
CAMBRIDGESHIRE,
28 SEPTEMBER 1974

OTHER CLUBS:
ROTHERHAM UNITED,
SOUTHEND UNITED,
CARLISLE UNITED,
STEVENAGE

Shaw was at his strongest playing in the hole behind a main attacker. In the run-in of the 1996–97 season, he started his first match for Arsenal in a Premiership clash at Southampton, where he scored a key goal. However, with the likes of Dennis Bergkamp, and Ian Wright also competing for a place in the starting line-up, Shaw was released.

In his nine-game Arsenal career, Clarke enthusiastically took on defenders, but for all his ability, there was a suspicion that he lacked the confidence and dedication to make it on the Premiership stage. After loan spells with Rotherham and Southend, he joined the Essex club full-time before dropping to non-league level.

MATTHEW
ROSE

LEE
HARPER

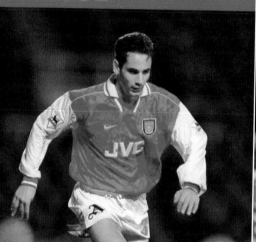

MATTHEW ROSE
(1995/96–1996/97)

POSITION:
DEFENDER

APPEARANCES:
5

BORN:
DARTFORD, KENT,
24 SEPTEMBER 1975

OTHER CLUBS:
QUEEN'S PARK
RANGERS,
YEOVIL TOWN

LEE HARPER
(1996/97)

POSITION:
GOALKEEPER

APPEARANCES:
1

BORN:
CHELSEA, LONDON,
30 OCTOBER 1971

OTHER CLUBS:
QUEEN'S PARK
RANGERS, WALSALL,
NORTHAMPTON
TOWN, MK DONS

Matthew Rose captained the side that won the FA Youth Cup in 1994. During his few run-outs for the first-team, Rose appeared to be an adaptable, fast defender with reasonable passing ability. In May 1997, he was sold to Queen's Park Rangers where he has became an incredibly popular figure, making over 250 appearances for the West London club.

Lee Harper, having been plucked from relative obscurity, made just one appearance for Arsenal. This, however, would be enough to secure his place in the record books. Thanks to the clean sheet he kept in that match – a 2-0 victory over Southampton, he has a 100 per cent record as an Arsenal goalkeeper.

REMI GARDE

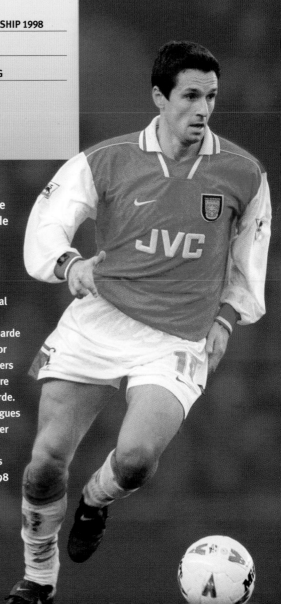

REMI GARDE
(1996/97–1998/99)

POSITION:
DEFENDER/MIDFIELDER

APPEARANCES:
43

BORN:
L'ARBRESLE, FRANCE,
3 APRIL 1966

CLUB HONOURS:
LEAGUE CHAMPIONSHIP 1998

OTHER HONOURS:
6 FRANCE CAPS

OTHER CLUBS:
LYON, STRASBOURG

In every Club's history, there are players who are valued by the supporters for the quiet but significant contribution they made to the cause, but who are less recognized further afield.

Remi Garde, one of the two players who arrived as Wenger purchases before the new manager took his place in the dug-out, is typical of this genre.

Versatile, professional, and very assured, Garde played at full-back, centre-back and midfield for Arsenal. If ever a dictionary of Arsenal footballers is made, under the heading of 'competent', there will be a photograph of the aptly-sounding Garde. He was known for guiding his defensive colleagues to another clean sheet and for prompting further positive play from the middle of the park.

The likes of Bergkamp, Vieira and Overmars made the headlines as Arsenal won the 1997–98 Double, but Garde was responsible for many of those all-important positive paragraphs underneath. His experience and adaptability were priceless throughout the campaign.

DENNIS BERGKAMP

'We've got Dennis Bergkamp, we've got Dennis Bergkamp.' Arsenal fans sung this song with joy and enthusiasm throughout the Dutchman's 10 years at the Club.

DENNIS BERGKAMP (1995/96–2005/06)	CLUB HONOURS: LEAGUE CHAMPIONSHIP 1998, 2002, 2004; FA CUP 1998, 2002, 2003, 2005
POSITION: STRIKER	
APPEARANCES: 423	OTHER HONOURS: 79 HOLLAND CAPS (37 GOALS)
GOALS: 120	OTHER CLUBS: AJAX, INTER MILAN
BORN: AMSTERDAM, HOLLAND, 10 MAY 1969	

The supporters sung it not just as a celebration or a boast, but also as self-reassurance that what was happening was real. When Bergkamp arrived at the Club in 1995, few Gunners fans could believe their luck that the famous Dutch master was now an Arsenal player.

Having scored 75 goals in 91 games for Ajax, Bergkamp seemed set to become a Serie A star when he signed for Inter Milan in 1993. However, he never played to anywhere near his peak in Italy. When he arrived at Highbury two years later, he needed a new challenge and Arsenal desperately needed a morale boost following a traumatic season.

Both parties got what they wanted – and more. Breathtakingly gifted, Bergkamp showed the sort of deft control of a ball that had made him one of the planet's most celebrated stars. Probing and controlling the attack from a withdrawn position, his vision and speed of thought meant he created openings where few other players would have seen them.

His third season with the Club saw him take this brilliance to a new level. Bergkamp won both the PFA and Football Writers' Player of the Year awards and he became the first player for 25 years to claim first, second and third places in the BBC's Goal of the Month competition, following his hat-trick of wonder strikes at Leicester City. Most crucially, he walked away with a Premiership medal.

Arsenal fans would have to wait four years for Bergkamp to really fizz again but when he did, the Club won another Double. The memorable moment of the 2001–02 campaign came with the Dutch international's goal at St James' Park. Although approaching his 35th birthday, he was influential as the Club claimed its unbeaten championship in 2004.

During his final season, Arsenal had themed match days to mark the final campaign at Highbury. One theme was Dennis Bergkamp day and he duly scored that day, against WBA. He signed off with his testimonial against Ajax, the first match at Emirates Stadium.

'HIS VISION AND SPEED OF THOUGHT MEANT HE CREATED OPENINGS WHERE FEW OTHER PLAYERS WOULD HAVE SEEN THEM'

As you would expect from a Club that has enjoyed such success during the Premiership era, Arsenal players have amassed many personal awards. With football writers, fans, television viewers and the players themselves voting for various football awards, there have been plenty to go around in the Arsenal dressing room!

▲ *Dennis Bergkamp – Goal of the season 2002/03*

THE ROLL OF HONOUR

THE PFA PLAYERS' PLAYER OF THE YEAR

Members of the Professional Footballers' Association (PFA) vote on this award. It was first presented in 1974.

Dennis Bergkamp (1998)

The Dutchman enjoyed an extraordinary season and was highly influential as the Club stormed to the Double. This was the first time an Arsenal player had won the award since Liam Brady collected it in 1979.

Thierry Henry (2003, 2004)

In 2003, Henry beat off the challenge of fellow nominee strikers Gianfranco Zola, Alan Shearer, Ruud van Nistelrooy and James Beattie to land this award. In 2004, he won it again after his 29 goals in 37 appearances spearheaded Arsenal's drive to the Premiership title. 'This award is very pleasing for me and rounds off a brilliant season', he smiled. Thierry Henry was the first player to win this award in two consecutive seasons.

THE PFA YOUNG PLAYER OF THE YEAR

This award is also voted for by members of the PFA. Any player under the age of 23 in the English leagues is eligible for it.

Nicolas Anelka (1999)

Having fired the Gunners to the Double in 1997–98, Anelka was on explosive form again the following season, scoring 17 goals in 34 league appearances. The young Frenchman said: 'It is a great honour for me to receive this highly regarded accolade and I would now like to take the opportunity to thank my fellow professionals for voting for me'.

THE PFA FANS PLAYER OF THE YEAR

Voted for by football supporters, this completes the hat-trick of PFA-related awards.

Thierry Henry (2003, 2004)

By receiving this award in the same two years that he won the PFA award voted for by the players, Henry proved that the players and the fans can see the game the same way! PFA chief executive Gordon Taylor said: 'Thierry is poetry in motion'.

THE FOOTBALL WRITERS' ASSOCIATION PLAYER OF THE YEAR

First awarded in 1948, this is voted for by members of the Football Writers' Association.

Dennis Bergkamp (1998)

The fourth successive overseas player to win the award, Bergkamp was the first Arsenal player to win since Frank McLintock, captain of the double-winning side of 1970–71.

Robert Pires (2002)

As he prepared to undergo surgery on the knee injury that curtailed his season, Pires was cheered by the news that he had won. He said: 'Obviously, it is a great honour for me. I know how important it is in English football'.

▲ *Thierry Henry – Players' Player of the year 2003*

Thierry Henry (2003, 2004, 2006)

In 2003, Henry became the 11th Frenchman to win thanks not just to his goals, but his all-round flair. In 2006 he completed a unique hat-trick and said: 'What I am especially proud of is that I am the first person to win the Footballer of the Year trophy three times. It is always pleasing to be the first to achieve something – it's a little piece of history'. Arsène Wenger commented: 'I think it is remarkable what he has done. He is the best scorer and best provider – so the choice is quite obvious this season'.

GOAL OF THE SEASON

This award has been decided by viewers of the BBC's Match of the Day and ITV's The Premiership show, depending on which channel showed Premiership football in each season.

Dennis Bergkamp (1997–98, 2001–02)

The first award was for his hat-trick strike against Leicester City at Filbert Street on 27 August 1997. In injury-time, David Platt floated a pass to Bergkamp who was in the penalty area. The Dutchman controlled the ball perfectly with his right foot, flicked it inside Matt Elliott with his left, and tapped it into the top corner to complete his hat-trick.

The second award was for his mesmerizing goal at Newcastle United on 2 March 2002. Robert Pires found Bergkamp with his back to goal. He expertly controlled the ball despite the close attention of Nikos Dabizas, flicked the ball to his right, spun round to meet it, and with the defender beaten, slotted it home.

Thierry Henry (2002–03)

Henry ran the length of the pitch before scoring this goal against Tottenham Hotspur on 16 November 2002. He then ran all the way back to celebrate it! There were more celebrations for Henry when it was voted goal of the season.

DAVID PLATT

It is strange to recall now but, for some Arsenal fans, the arrival of David Platt during the summer of 1995 promised an even more tantalizing prospect than the signing of Dennis Bergkamp the same summer.

DAVID PLATT
(1995/96–1997/98)
POSITION:
MIDFIELDER
APPEARANCES:
108
GOALS:
15
BORN:
CHADDERTON, LANCASHIRE, 10 JUNE 1966

CLUB HONOURS:
LEAGUE CHAMPIONSHIP 1998; FA CUP 1998
OTHER HONOURS:
62 ENGLAND CAPS (27 GOALS)
OTHER CLUBS:
CREWE ALEXANDRA, ASTON VILLA, BARI, JUVENTUS, SAMPDORIA, NOTTINGHAM FOREST
MANAGERIAL CAREER:
SAMPDORIA, NOTTINGHAM FOREST, ENGLAND UNDER 21

For some years, goals from the middle of the park had been rarities at Highbury, and so the arrival of the prolific David Platt raised great expectations in North London. He had scored 51 goals in 121 matches for Aston Villa and had also enjoyed an illustrious England career, scoring a key goal in the 1990 World Cup Finals and often wearing the captain's armband.

Fast forward to his third season with Arsenal, when Platt rose to nod a memorable and vital winner against Manchester United during the Double-winning campaign, and all seems to be going to script. However, the intervening period had seen a narrative that wasn't quite as expected.

During Platt's first two seasons with Arsenal, the midfielder – who had starred in Italy for Bari, Juventus and Sampdoria – was not able to impress as consistently as he would have liked. That said, Platt and his fellow summer-signing Bergkamp, scored a vital goal each in the victory over Bolton Wanderers that secured European football for his second Highbury campaign.

However, it was Platt's third season where the former England captain's character, ability and professionalism shone most brightly. Although Patrick Vieira, Emmanuel Petit and Ray Parlour had the midfield places tied up, Platt was his usual dignified and professional self whenever called upon, and he made 14 starts and 26 appearances from the bench.

On a lively November Sunday afternoon at Highbury, Arsenal and Manchester United had shared four goals when the home side won a corner-kick late in the match. What a fitting reward for Platt as he rose to nod the ball home, sending the home fans into delirium, and providing a key twist in what was to prove a memorable campaign.

Platt left the Club in the summer of 1998 and has since enjoyed coaching spells at club level in England and Italy and also with the England Under-21s. He is also a regular pundit on television.

'WHAT A FITTING REWARD FOR PLATT AS HE ROSE TO NOD THE BALL HOME ... A KEY TWIST IN A MEMORABLE CAMPAIGN'

NICOLAS ANELKA

The controversy that plagued Nicolas Anelka's exit from Arsenal must not be allowed to cloud the contributions he made at Highbury, most notably the part he played in the 1998 Double triumph.

NICOLAS ANELKA (1996/97–1998/99)	CLUB HONOURS: LEAGUE CHAMPIONSHIP 1998; FA CUP 1998
POSITION: STRIKER	OTHER HONOURS: 38 FRANCE CAPS (10 GOALS)
APPEARANCES: 90	OTHER CLUBS: PARIS ST GERMAIN,
GOALS: 28	REAL MADRID, LIVERPOOL, MANCHESTER CITY,
BORN: VERSAILLES, FRANCE, 14 MARCH 1979	FENERBAHCE, BOLTON WANDERERS

Nicolas Anelka was unheard of when he arrived in England in March 1997, but the public already trusted Arsène Wenger when he indicated that he had acquired someone special. However, the 17-year-old Anelka struggled to impose himself during his first nine months at the Club. He was known more for his tendency to stray offside than for goals.

When Ian Wright was injured, the youngster's time had come. Even for a Club like Arsenal, Doubles do not come along very often and are to be treasured. As the Double-chasing Gunners sped towards the finishing line, Anelka was at the front of the red and white pack.

The final months of the season were nervous for many, but the Frenchman seemed to grow in assurance. His contribution was crowned with a fine strike in the FA Cup Final against Newcastle United.

During the 1998–99 season he continued to terrorize defenders, but concern was already growing over his attitude. Anelka had rarely seemed to share much warmth with his team-mates and his smiles were few and far between. Sure enough, that summer he left the Club for Real Madrid.

Anelka has not settled anywhere for long since leaving North London and it has been disappointing to see a player who was once tipped for world-class status fail to live up to his early promise. It is difficult not to conclude that had Anelka stayed at Arsenal under the eye of Wenger, he may have reached a much higher level, especially if he had partnered Thierry Henry for Club as well as country.

He has since played for three other English clubs. With both Liverpool and Manchester City he showed regular glimpses of the fine form that he showed at Highbury. In 2006 he joined Bolton Wanderers and duly scored twice against Arsenal in a match at the Reebok Stadium. Could the Frenchman return to the heights that marked his first full season in English football?

'HAD ANELKA STAYED AT ARSENAL UNDER THE EYE OF WENGER, HE MAY HAVE REACHED A MUCH HIGHER LEVEL'

As you would expect from a team full of stars who win so consistently at Club level, Arsenal's dressing room has boasted many players who have lifted trophies at international level. From the French connection which has enjoyed plentiful success on the international stage, to an African ace and a couple of brilliant Brazilians, Gunners stars have conquered many an international football summit during the Premiership years...

▲ *Arsenal's Copa America winner Julio Baptista*

WORLD-CLASS GUNNERS!

THE 1998 WORLD CUP

On their home soil, the French went from strength to strength in the competition and ended up winning the trophy. There was much joy to be had for strikers who either already were, or would soon become, Arsenal players. A young winger named Thierry Henry was France's top scorer, while the tournament's leading scorer overall was the Croatian future Gunner Davor Suker. However, perhaps the most memorable goal was scored by Dennis Bergkamp against Argentina in the quarter-finals.

France beat Brazil in the Final. For the crowning goal, Patrick Vieira fed Emmanuel Petit to slot home, prompting a memorable newspaper headline the following day: "Arsenal Win The World Cup!"

ARSENAL MEDAL-WINNERS: THIERRY HENRY, EMMANUEL PETIT, PATRICK VIEIRA, ROBERT PIRES

THE 2000 AFRICA CUP OF NATIONS & OLYMPIC GAMES

Lauren's Cameroon marched to the final of this competition, where they faced a tough challenge in co-hosts Nigeria in February 2000. The tie ended 2-2 and went to a penalty shoot-out. Cameroon won 4-3 on penalties.

Later that year, Cameroon faced Spain in the Men's Olympic Football Final at the Olympic Stadium in Sydney. Once again, the game ended 2-2 after extra-time and a penalty shoot-out was needed to separate the teams. Lauren successfully converted Cameroon's fourth and his team won the shoot-out 5-3.

ARSENAL MEDAL-WINNER: LAUREN

▶ *Patrick Vieira, a 1998 World Cup and 2000 European Championship winner, shoots the final penalty at the 2005 FA Cup Final*

THE 2000 EUROPEAN CHAMPIONSHIP

Having lifted the World Cup in 1998, France had no intentions of taking it easy in this, their next international tournament. Once again, Thierry Henry was their leading scorer as they reached the Final. There, they faced Italy who were winning 1-0 until the last minute of a tense match. Then, substitute and future Gunner Sylvain Wiltord struck a sweet equalizer for the French. In extra-time, France grabbed the golden goal to win the tournament.

ARSENAL MEDAL-WINNERS: THIERRY HENRY, SYLVAIN WILTORD, EMMANUEL PETIT, ROBERT PIRES, PATRICK VIEIRA.

THE 2002 WORLD CUP

He was a late addition to the Brazil squad but Gilberto ended up playing in every minute of each of his national team's games in the tournament and consequently arrived at Highbury with a winners' medal in his pocket. Gilberto was awesome in the final when Brazil beat Germany 2-0. He and his team-mates won all six of their ties and were the first team to do this since the legendary Brazilians of 1970.

ARSENAL MEDAL-WINNER: GILBERTO

THE 2004 COPA AMERICA

Held in Peru, this tournament was won by a Brazilian side including Arsenal midfielder Gilberto and future Gunner Julio Baptista. The team had a tricky route to the Final and needed penalty shoot-outs to separate them from Uruguay in the semi-final and Argentina in the Final.

PATRICK VIEIRA

Formidable, immense and imperious: even these words seem to fall short of describing just how vital a presence Patrick Vieira was in the Arsenal team during his eight years with the Club.

PATRICK VIEIRA (1996/97–2004/05)	CLUB HONOURS: LEAGUE CHAMPIONSHIP 1998, 2002, 2004; FA CUP 1998, 2002, 2005
POSITION: MIDFIELDER	
APPEARANCES: 407	OTHER HONOURS: 101 FRANCE CAPS (6 GOALS)
GOALS: 34	OTHER CLUBS: CANNES, AC MILAN, JUVENTUS, INTER MILAN
BORN: DAKAR, SENEGAL, 23 JUNE 1976	

This colossal, dogged and talented man was quite literally the heart of the side. The first signing made by Arsène Wenger, Vieira arrived at the Club before Wenger officially took the reins and he was a superb ambassador for the new manager. Coming on as a substitute against Sheffield Wednesday in 1996, he showed skill, determination and commitment. Rarely has a new signing been so quickly taken to the supporters' hearts.

The Senegal-born midfielder dictated not just the flow of the play in the middle of the park; he also determined the tempo of the entire game. Following a biting tackle, he would speed down the field to set up another assault for his illustrious attacking colleagues.

He had disciplinary problems in his early years with the Club, but he worked on his temperament and soon improved his behaviour.

Having starred when Arsenal won the 1998 and 2002 Doubles, he was quite naturally named as Tony Adams's replacement as captain. Though the two played in different positions, when this tall, confident young man led out The Gunners, he was an absolutely appropriate and worthy successor to Adams.

The captain during the 49-match unbeaten run, Vieira also opened the scoring at White Hart Lane on the day The Gunners clinched the 2004 Premiership title. This was a fitting moment of glory for the man who had engineered so much of Arsenal's success. He had been magnificent throughout the campaign, never more so than in the victory at Chelsea in February. In a highly charged match, Vieira was in thunderous, dominant form and capped a fine performance with a goal.

However, his final moment of glory came in the 2005 FA Cup Final when he stroked home the decisive spot-kick in the penalty shoot-out. It was the last ball he kicked in an Arsenal shirt. It had been feared that Vieira would leave the club, and he did in the summer of 2005 to join Juventus.

'HE DICTATED NOT JUST THE FLOW OF THE PLAY IN THE MIDDLE OF THE PARK; HE ALSO DETERMINED THE TEMPO OF THE ENTIRE GAME'

GILLES GRIMANDI

GILLES GRIMANDI
(1997/98–2001/02)
POSITION:
DEFENDER/MIDFIELDER
APPEARANCES:
170
GOALS:
7
BORN:
GAP, FRANCE,
11 NOVEMBER 1970

CLUB HONOURS:
LEAGUE CHAMPIONSHIP 1998,
2002; FA CUP 1998, 2002
OTHER CLUBS:
MONACO

Arsène Wenger had been Arsenal manager for less than a year when he signed Gilles Grimandi, who stayed with the Club for the remainder of his playing career.

Following his retirement as a player, Grimandi was then recalled by Wenger who wanted him to scout for the Club. Wenger's huge faith in the Gap-born utility player speaks volumes for his ability and professional character. Not many would have predicted during Grimandi's first few months with Arsenal that player and Club would go on to have such a long-standing and successful relationship. Covering for Tony Adams in the centre of defence, the Frenchman did not look like a traditional centre-back, and a few crucial moments of inattention were highlighted by his critics.

However, by the end of the Double-winning season, his contribution – including a crucial match-winner in a tight match against Crystal Palace – was recognized. During his subsequent years with the Club, Grimandi played as a centre-back, full-back and central midfielder.

The affection he was held in by his team-mates and his manager show that Grimandi was very much a players' player. He was extremely popular in the stands, too.

CHRISTOPHER WREH

CHRISTOPHER WREH
(1997/98–2000/01)
POSITION:
STRIKER
APPEARANCES:
46
GOALS:
5
BORN:
**MONROVIA, LIBERIA,
14 MAY 1975**

CLUB HONOURS:
**LEAGUE CHAMPIONSHIP 1998;
FA CUP 1998**
OTHER CLUBS:
**MONACO, AEK ATHENS,
BIRMINGHAM CITY, DEN BOSCH,
AL-HILAL, ST MIRREN**

Wreh arrived from Monaco late in the close-season and it took some months for him to show his worth. Once he did, he was not lacking in admirers among the Arsenal faithful.

As a striker, Wreh had it all: he could shoot and assist with equal accuracy and he was powerful and fast. He even had a special celebration; doing somersaults in the air. His calm demeanour was just what the doctor ordered during that season.

For the clubs contesting the championship, the closing months of the football season can be nerve-wracking. However, if Christopher Wreh found the run-in to the victorious 1997–98 season tense, he certainly didn't show it.

Crucial goals against Bolton Wanderers and Wimbledon in the league and against Wolverhampton Wanderers in the FA Cup semi-final mean that Arsenal's second Double would not have been secured without the Liberian-born striker's contribution. No longer did he labour in the shadow of his cousin – and fellow Wenger protegé – George Weah. Sadly, he didn't build on this and left the Club in 2000.

EMMANUEL PETIT

When Emmanuel Petit and Patrick Vieira exchanged their customary 'high-five' salute just before the start of a match, it was enough to shoot adrenalin through the body of any Arsenal supporter who witnessed it.

EMMANUEL PETIT
(1997/98–1999/2000)

POSITION:
MIDFIELDER

APPEARANCES:
118

GOALS:
11

BORN:
DIEPPE, FRANCE,
22 SEPTEMBER 1970

CLUB HONOURS:
LEAGUE CHAMPIONSHIP 1997/98;
FA CUP 1997/98

OTHER HONOURS:
63 FRANCE CAPS (6 GOALS)

OTHER CLUBS:
MONACO, BARCELONA, CHELSEA

The pair were simply formidable for Arsenal. So much so that it is easy to forget the doubts that surrounded Petit during his first months in North London.

Petit was reunited with Arsène Wenger – who had managed him at Monaco – in 1997. In the early months of his first season, many fans felt that Petit's contribution was disappointing, especially considering the expectations surrounding him since his arrival from Monaco. The Frenchman had spent much of his career in defence and some wondered if Wenger had been wise to move him into the midfield.

As we have learned so often since, to question Wenger's judgement is nearly always foolish, and so it proved with his deployment of Petit. Following a crucial team meeting in the autumn of 1997, the transformation of the French international was incredible. He and Vieira formed an exceptional partnership; both played with tenacious energy and with merciless ability in the tackle. They could also supply a telling pass for their colleagues.

As the run-in to the Club's second Double gathered pace, Petit became respected and feared by opponents, and utterly idolized by the Arsenal faithful. His first goal for the Club came during a 5-0 demolition of Wimbledon in April 1998 but it was greeted as if it were the winner in a Champions League Final, such was the love that he had inspired in his supporters. More crucially, it was his wonderfully judged pass that set up Marc Overmars to open the scoring in the FA Cup Final against Newcastle United the following month.

Two goals, two medals, and heartfelt respect from the Arsenal fans; the first half of 1998 had been good for Petit. The year got better when he scored the crowning goal in France's World Cup Final victory over Brazil.

During the following two campaigns, his increased profile made him a targeted man and he was forced to run a gauntlet of provocative and brutal challenges from opponents. He continued to perform excellently, but seemed unhappy and moved to Barcelona in 2000.

‘PETIT BECAME
RESPECTED AND FEARED
BY OPPONENTS, AND
UTTERLY IDOLIZED BY
THE ARSENAL FAITHFUL’

MATTHEW UPSON

MATTHEW UPSON
(1997/98–2002/03)

POSITION:
DEFENDER

APPEARANCES:
56

BORN:
HARTISMERE, SUFFOLK,
18 APRIL 1979

CLUB HONOURS:
LEAGUE CHAMPIONSHIP 2002

OTHER HONOURS:
7 ENGLAND CAPS

OTHER CLUBS:
LUTON TOWN, NOTTINGHAM
FOREST, CRYSTAL PALACE,
READING, BIRMINGHAM CITY,
WEST HAM UNITED

The Gunners spent £1m on Matthew Upson when he had made only one professional appearance as a substitute for Luton Town.

It is not surprising, therefore, that expectation and curiosity were in the air when he arrived at the Club in the summer of 1997. An assured, pacey defender, Upson had the added advantage of being extremely able with his left foot. He moved quickly from the reserves to the first team and made a handful of impressive performances during the latter stages of the 1997–98 season as the Gunners tied up the Club's second Double.

However, three major obstacles stood in his way to first-team regularity and their names were Adams, Bould and Keown. His best chance came in the 2001–02 seasons when the departure of Bould some seasons back and injuries to the other two gave him a clean run. However, as fate would have it, he suffered a knee injury and circumstances were never as positive for him again. Understandably, Upson soon decided he had to look elsewhere and in 2003 the inevitable happened when he was sold to Birmingham City, the Club he had made his Arsenal debut against. He has since moved to West Ham.

LUIS BOA MORTE

LUIS BOA MORTE **(1997/98–1999/2000)**	**CLUB HONOURS:** **LEAGUE CHAMPIONSHIP 1998**
POSITION: **STRIKER**	**OTHER HONOURS:** **25 PORTUGAL CAPS (2 GOALS)**
APPEARANCES: **39**	**OTHER CLUBS:** **SOUTHAMPTON, FULHAM,**
GOALS: **4**	**WEST HAM UNITED**
BORN: **LISBON, PORTUGAL,** **4 AUGUST 1977**	

Given his, at times, eye-catching style of play, it is ironic that Luis Boa Morte had to bide his time and wait for his stock to rise in English football.

However, Boa Morte is now recognized as an important Premiership player. One of a clutch of players acquired during the summer of 1997, he did not star in the subsequent Double-winning campaign to the same extent as some of the other new purchases. However, the pacey and dynamic winger made enough starts to win a Premiership medal and to catch the attention in the early rounds of the FA Cup and League Cup.

There was never any doubting his natural ability and enthusiasm, but his form could be erratic and his eagerness to impress sometimes showed itself at the expense of the team ethos. However, several performances stand out, not least his goal-scoring appearance against Panathinaikos in 1998.

The arrival of Nwankwo Kanu, Thierry Henry and Davor Suker made competition for places extremely keen, and in August 1999 Boa Morte joined Southampton, the team he made his Arsenal debut against.

MARC OVERMARS

When Arsène Wenger explained his purchase of Marc Overmars in 1997, he said 'he had something to prove'. The Dutch winger proved his point in style, and did so immediately.

MARC OVERMARS 1997/98–1999/2000	CLUB HONOURS: LEAGUE CHAMPIONSHIP 1998; FA CUP 1998
POSITION: MIDFIELDER	**OTHER HONOURS:** 74 HOLLAND CAPS (17 GOALS)
APPEARANCES: 142	**OTHER CLUBS:** GO AHEAD EAGLES, WILLEM II, AJAX, BARCELONA
GOALS: 41	
BORN: EMST, HOLLAND, 29 MARCH 1973	

Wenger said; 'When I did my homework on him I discovered he was upset at the rumours he was not fit and that he could never play to his true ability again. That was a good sign for me, a hurt player. He had something to prove.'

Overmars' contribution to the 1998 Double can scarcely be overestimated. As he lashed the ball past Peter Schmeichel at Old Trafford in March, he scored the season's most iconic goal and one which truly tipped the balance in favour of Arsenal. He also opened the scoring in the FA Cup Final against Newcastle, and proved the cynics wrong.

Overmars had suffered a serious cruciate ligament injury and there had been whispered suggestions that he would never return to the heights he had reached in his mid-20s with some dazzling displays for the national side. However, as with a number of Wenger purchases including Thierry Henry and Emmanuel Petit, the former Ajax star used Arsenal to reboot a career that had lost some of its fizz.

A no-nonsense winger, Overmars was not interested in step-overs or other extravagances. He was too busy racing towards goal either with the ball at his feet or with the expectation of completing someone else's run with one of his trademark cool finishes. The lightning-quick winger was often double-marked, offering valuable extra space to the strikers.

Although he never regained the heights of his first season with the Club, Overmars remained utterly committed to the Arsenal cause and could still raise the Highbury crowd out of their seats during his last two years in North London. In the summer of 2000, he moved on to a new big-club challenge with Barcelona.

Sadly, in the summer of 2004, Overmars was forced to retire from the game at the age of just 31 due to a persistent knee injury. It was an upsetting early end to a fine career. However, he had more than repaid the faith that Wenger had shown in him and endeared himself to the Arsenal faithful.

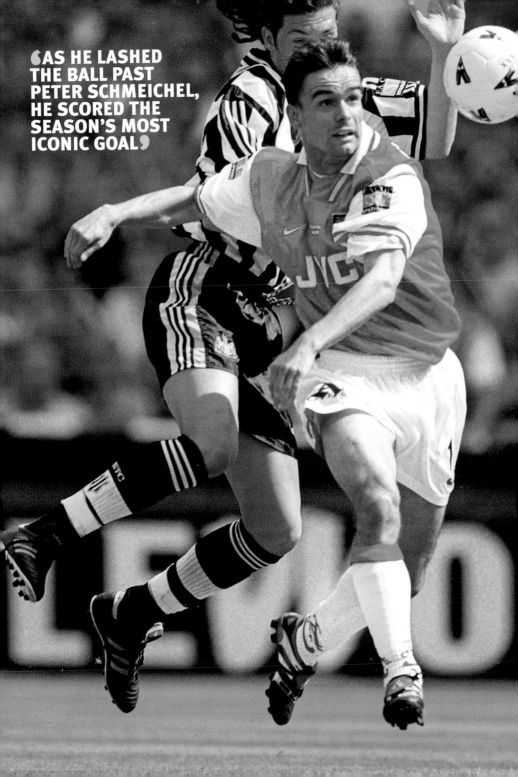

‘AS HE LASHED
THE BALL PAST
PETER SCHMEICHEL,
HE SCORED THE
SEASON'S MOST
ICONIC GOAL’

ALBERTO
MENDEZ

PAOLO
VERNAZZA

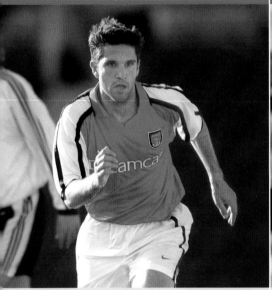

ALBERTO MENDEZ
(1997/98–2001/02)
POSITION:
MIDFIELDER
APPEARANCES:
11
GOALS:
2
BORN:
NUREMBERG,
GERMANY,
24 OCTOBER 1974

OTHER CLUBS:
FC FEUCHT,
AEK ATHENS,
SPV UNTERHACKING

PAOLO VERNAZZA
(1997/98–2000/01)
POSITION:
MIDFIELDER
APPEARANCES:
12
GOALS:
1
BORN:
ISLINGTON, LONDON,
1 NOVEMBER 1979

OTHER CLUBS:
IPSWICH TOWN,
PORTSMOUTH,
WATFORD,
ROTHERHAM,
BARNET,
DAGENHAM,
REDBRIDGE

Arsène Wenger signed Alberto Mendez having watched him play just one match for German fifth division side FC Feucht. Due in part to bad luck with injuries, Mendez never did enough to prove the Frenchman's gamble was justified by truly impressing for Arsenal. He has since played in the Greek and Spanish leagues.

An accurate passer with an imaginative mind, Vernazza's play was easy on the eye. However, he was only given occasional run-outs, often from the substitute's bench, so he was unable to prove whether his gifts could be handed out on a regular basis. His only goal for Arsenal came against Coventry City three months before he left the Club.

DAVID
GRONDIN

FABIAN
CABALLERO

DAVID GRONDIN
(1998/99–2002/03)
POSITION:
DEFENDER
APPEARANCES:
4
BORN:
PARIS, FRANCE,
8 MAY 1980

OTHER CLUBS:
CANNES,
DUNFERMLINE
ATHLETIC

FABIAN CABALLERO
(1998/99)
POSITION:
FORWARD
APPEARANCES:
3
BORN:
MISIONES,
ARGENTINA,
31 JANUARY 1978

OTHER CLUBS:
CERRO PORTINO,
CLUB SOL DE
AMERICA,
DUNDEE,
OLIMPIA ASUNCION,
TACUARY,
DAEJEON CITIZEN

Grondin could play in a number of positions in defence and could also deputize in midfield. He made his debut in the League Cup clash with Derby County in October 1998. He only managed three more appearances for the Gunners before he was loaned to Cannes and then sold to Dunfermline Athletic.

Making only three appearances for the Gunners, Argentine Fabian Caballero never made any of his contributions register on the Richter scale. After his loan spell expired at the end of the 1998–99 season, he returned to the Paraguayan league and then came back to the UK to play with Dundee, where he scored seven goals in his first 18 matches.

ALEX
MANNINGER

ALEX MANNINGER
(1997/98–2001/02)

POSITION:
GOALKEEPER

APPEARANCES:
64

BORN:
SALZBURG, AUSTRIA,
4 JUNE 1977

CLUB HONOURS:
LEAGUE CHAMPIONSHIP 1998

OTHER HONOURS:
19 AUSTRIA CAPS

OTHER CLUBS:
SALZBURG, STEYR, CASINO GRAZ,
FIORENTINA, RCD ESPANYOL,
TORINO, BRESCIA, SIENA,
RED BULL SALZBURG

Such had been the glory of David Seaman's reign, when he was injured during the second half of the 1997–98 season, few were confident when an unknown young Austrian emerged to replace him.

Within months, Alex Manninger was being credited as playing a significant role in the Club's second Double, and some were asking how long it would be until he ousted Seaman from the first team for good.

Among the six Premiership clean sheets he kept that season was one at Old Trafford which came as a result of a number of breathtaking saves. An FA Cup triumph at Upton Park came after a penalty shoot-out. It was fitting that the youngster received a Premiership medal despite not playing the requisite number of matches.

In England, the fairy tale was not to continue. Seaman's absences were few and far between during 1998–99, and although he was injured the following season, he returned to first team action and Manninger had to return to the bench. He had performed well as stand-in, but questions over his concentration levels had meant that it was a foregone conclusion that Seaman would return once fit. Manninger left Arsenal for Fiorentina in 2002.

ISAIAH RANKIN

IGORS STEPANOVS

ISAIAH RANKIN	OTHER CLUBS:
(1996/97–1997/98)	COLCHESTER UNITED,
POSITION:	BRADFORD CITY,
STRIKER	BIRMINGHAM CITY,
APPEARANCES:	BOLTON WANDERERS,
1	BARNSLEY, GRIMSBY,
BORN:	BRENTFORD,
EDMONTON, LONDON,	MACCLESFIELD TOWN
22 MAY 1978	

IGORS STEPANOVS	OTHER HONOURS:
(2000/01–2003/04)	92 LATVIA CAPS
POSITION:	(3 GOALS)
DEFENDER	**OTHER CLUBS:**
APPEARANCES:	SKONTO RIGA,
31	BEVEREN,
GOALS:	GRASSHOPPER,
1	FK JURMALA,
BORN:	ESBJERG
OGRE, LATVIA,	
21 JANUARY 1976	

After some attention-grabbing form for the reserves, nippy striker Isaiah Rankin was promoted to the first-team bench in May 1997 having scoring a fantastic 68 goals in 114 youth and reserve team appearances. The young man clearly had talent, but apart from one appearance against Tottenham Hotspur, Rankin couldn't get a first-team place.

Having started well with Arsenal, the Latvian endured an awful afternoon in February 2001 when the team were beaten 6-1 at Old Trafford. A year later, Stepanovs was awarded another run in the team due to injuries. The Gunners were heading for another Double and the defender truly bounced back with some fine performances.

FREDRIK LJUNGBERG

It is said that first impressions count so Freddie Ljungberg did well to lob Peter Schmeichel just seconds into his Arsenal debut. It was an admirable strike and throughout his subsequent years with the Club, Ljungberg showed that it was no flash in the pan.

FREDRIK LJUNGBERG
(1998/99–PRESENT)
POSITION:
MIDFIELDER
APPEARANCES:
328
GOALS:
72
BORN:
**VITTSJO, SWEDEN,
16 APRIL 1977**

CLUB HONOURS:
**LEAGUE CHAMPIONSHIP 2002,
2004; FA CUP 2002, 2003, 2005**
OTHER HONOURS:
67 SWEDEN CAPS (13 GOALS)
OTHER CLUBS:
HALMSTADS BK

His debut goal displayed a keen sense of timing and occasion, two qualities that the plucky midfielder has always had plentiful supplies of.

However, it was not until his second season with the Club that he began to really show his ability as a versatile and tireless midfielder. Then, in the 2001–02 season he positively excelled. He stabbed home a Pires pass to win a Premiership clash at Anfield in December, but this was merely a foretaste of the run-in when his six goals in five games confirmed the Gunners as champions.

He also scored in that season's 2-0 FA Cup Final victory over Chelsea, becoming the first man to score in successive finals for four decades with a curling shot from the edge of the penalty box. The following season, Freddie continued his love affair with the FA Cup when he hit the winner against Sheffield United in the FA Cup semi-final. Europe has also been a happy hunting ground for the Swede who loves to run for his side: he has scored against Inter Milan, Lokomotiv Moscow and hit a brace at home to Juventus.

Ljungberg's hairstyle became iconic with the Arsenal fans over the years – from a short and spiky effort, through a red Mohawk to the current cropped affair – as did his effervescent contributions to the Arsenal team. The squad and – with a new home – the Club itself now radically differs to when Ljungberg arrived in 1998. Freddie's form throughout these changing times was familiar and fantastic. He moved across the capital to West Ham United in the summer of 2007.

‘DURING THE 2001–02 RUN-IN HE WAS SUPERB AND HIS SIX GOALS IN FIVE GAMES CONFIRMED THE GUNNERS AS CHAMPIONS’

NELSON VIVAS

NELSON VIVAS
(1998/99–2000/01)

POSITION:
DEFENDER

APPEARANCES:
69

GOALS:
1

BORN:
GRANADERO BAIGORRIA,
ARGENTINA,
18 OCTOBER 1969

OTHER HONOURS:
39 ARGENTINA CAPS

OTHER CLUBS:
QUILMES, BOCA JUNIORS,
CELTA VIGO,
INTER MILAN

Sweeping into North London in the wake of the 1998 Double, Nelson Vivas looked like a man set for big things with Arsenal.

The Argentine international had superb positional sense, a tough tackle, and was a tidy passer of the ball. Vivas performed solidly, but, as Arsenal fans had come to expect, the famous back line were playing well.

When Silvinho and Luzhny were added to the mix the following summer, Vivas' position became even harder. He had never put a foot wrong for the Gunners, but he was soon on his way to Inter Milan.

SILVINHO

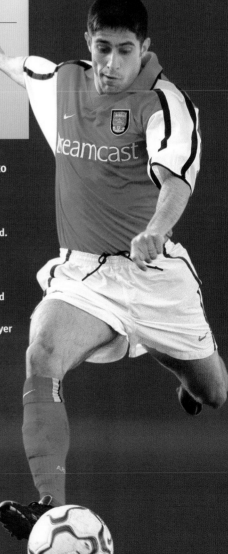

SILVINHO
(1999/2000–2000/01)

POSITION:
DEFENDER

APPEARANCES:
80

GOALS:
5

BORN:
**SAO PAULO, BRAZIL,
12 APRIL 1974**

OTHER CLUBS:
**CORINTHIANS, CELTA VIGO,
BARCELONA**

OTHER HONOURS:
6 BRAZIL CAPS

In the late 1990s, the Arsenal congregation began to wonder who would replace the 'famous four' back line that had served the team so well.

When supporters discovered that a Brazilian had been lined up to replace Nigel Winterburn, some were concerned. Would such a player be able to live up to the gritty determination of Winterburn?

You bet he could. Silvinho's attacking expertise could not be disputed. He loved to bomb forward at pace and had superb control of the ball. His crosses and corners were always dangerous too. However, the former Sao Paulo player could also defend brilliantly; his concentration, positional awareness, and wholehearted tackling eased any fears.

In May 2000, the Brazilian was on rampant form when Arsenal relegated Sheffield Wednesday. Although the Gunners conceded three goals during a balmy evening match, his long-range goal at the Clock End was typical of his vision. The result was 3-3.

Rarely has such a positive and happy fellow trodden the hallowed turf. The affection that he stirred among the fans is a measure of how neatly he deposed a Club legend. However, with the emergence of Ashley Cole, he moved to Celta Vigo.

NWANKWO KANU

The three goals scored by Nwankwo Kanu at Chelsea in 1999 is one of the key moments in Arsenal history and one of the most memorable hat-tricks of the Premiership era.

NWANKWO KANU
(1998/99–2003/04)
POSITION:
STRIKER
APPEARANCES:
198
GOALS:
44
BORN:
**OWERRI, NIGERIA,
1 AUGUST 1976**

CLUB HONOURS:
**LEAGUE CHAMPIONSHIP 2002,
2004; FA CUP 2002**
OTHER HONOURS:
66 NIGERIA CAPS (13 GOALS)
OTHER CLUBS:
**FEDERATION WORKS,
IWUANYANWU, AJAX, INTER
MILAN, WEST BROMWICH ALBION,
PORTSMOUTH**

In the last 17 minutes of the match, the Nigerian substitute gave Arsenal an unlikely victory with three fantastic goals. The third goal was the finest; a curling strike which Kanu unleashed from the byline and curled into the back of the net.

Wonder strikes are what Kanu will be remembered for. One was a breathtaking side-foot during the 6-1 victory over Middlesbrough in March 1999. Another was a memorable goal at Tottenham later that season, when Kanu gave Luke Young perhaps the most torrid 10 seconds of his career. This classic Kanu goal was cheeky, mesmerizing and completely unexpected, making the seemingly impossible appear simple.

Earlier in his life, Kanu had been diagnosed with a serious heart condition. Some doctors believed he might not live for long, and few would have given him a chance of continuing his career as a professional footballer. He struggled to pick up his career with Inter Milan following the diagnosis, but in 1999, Arsène Wenger – ever alert to the exciting potential of signing a player with something to prove – brought him to Highbury. The plan was to add some firepower to the Gunners as they tried to repeat the Double triumph of 1998.

At first sight, Kanu seemed a little too laid-back for the rigours of the Premiership. However, the Nigerian proved these fears to be comprehensively misjudged as he was soon dancing around defenders – and his goals in the closing stages of 1999 helped take Arsenal to the brink of further silverware.

In subsequent years, many of Kanu's appearances came from the bench and eventually he opted to move to West Bromwich Albion for a fresh challenge. During the 2006–07 season, he was an effective member of the Arsenal old boys side developing at Portsmouth Football Club.

'THE CLASSIC KANU GOAL WAS CHEEKY, MESMERIZING AND AROSE FROM CIRCUMSTANCES THAT MANY OTHER PLAYERS WOULD NOT CONSIDER FRUITFUL'

OLEG
LUZHNY

OLEG LUZHNY
(1999/2000–2002/03)
POSITION:
DEFENDER
APPEARANCES:
100
BORN:
LVIV, UKRAINE,
    5 AUGUST 1968

CLUB HONOURS:
LEAGUE CHAMPIONSHIP 2002;
FA CUP 2003
OTHER HONOURS:
8 USSR CAPS; 52 UKRAINE CAPS
OTHER CLUBS:
TORPEDO LUTSK, KARPATY LVIV,
DYNAMO KIEV, WOLVERHAMPTON
WANDERERS, FK VENTA

W e are used to short, nippy fellows filling the full-back positions in football, so it came as some surprise when Wenger signed a tall, stocky right-back who had been nicknamed 'the Horse'.

However, he proved to be a hugely competent defender with strength, pace, stamina and could deliver a deadly cross.

Not that Luzhny was an entirely unknown quantity when he signed for Arsenal in 1999. The previous season he had starred when Dynamo Kiev played the Gunners in the Champions League. He galloped – and rarely has that word been more appropriate – up and down the flank to great effect all evening. No wonder Wenger noticed him.

As it transpired, the imposing Ukrainian was to play not just at right-back, but in a number of positions during his Highbury years. His finest form in his first season came at centre-back. Luzhny subsequently also played at left-back, in addition to his preferred role on the other flank of the back four.

However, the brilliance of Lee Dixon coupled with the arrival of Lauren in 2000 kept Oleg out of the first team. In 2003 he moved to Wolverhampton Wanderers.

STEFAN
MALZ

KABA
DIAWARA

STEFAN
MALZ

KABA
DIAWARA

STEFAN MALZ
(1999/2000–2000/01)

POSITION:
MIDFIELDER

APPEARANCES:
14

GOALS:
2

BORN:
LUDWIGSHAFEN,
GERMANY,
15 JUNE 1972

OTHER CLUBS:
DARMSTADT 98,
VFR MANNHEIM,
TSV MUNICH 1860,
KAISERSLAUTERN

KABA DIAWARA
(1998/99)

POSITION:
STRIKER

APPEARANCES:
15

BORN:
TOULON, FRANCE,
16 DECEMBER, 1975

OTHER HONOURS:
GUINEA CAPS

OTHER CLUBS:
TOULON, BORDEAUX,
RENNES, MARSEILLES,
PARIS ST GERMAIN,
BLACKBURN ROVERS,
WEST HAM UNITED,
RACING DE FERROL,
NICE, AL-GHARAFFAH,
AL-KHARITIYATH,
AJACCIO,
GAZIANTEPSPOR

Stefan Malz did not grab his first-team opportunities with sufficient gusto to enter the reckoning for a regular spot. He did make some respectable shows in the League Cup, and scored two goals for the Club, most memorably at St James's Park in May 2000 when he shrugged off the close attention of Warren Barton to curl home a fine shot.

Signed from Bordeaux in January 1999, it was hoped that Diawara would add some fire to the Gunners' attack. Powerful, direct and energetic, the Toulon-born man had everything needed to do just that – apart from a bit of luck. He had no difficulty getting on the end of chances, but he could not convert his many shots into goals.

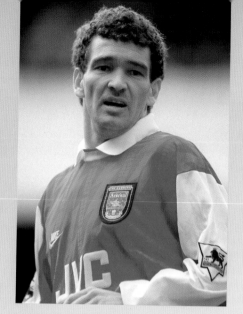

Most of the time, the players at a club like Arsenal, who win a special place in supporters' hearts, are also household names, admired by all those who follow the game.

However, all clubs have players who are loved by their own supporters but not necessarily for conventional reasons, and these players rarely receive much recognition beyond their own club. They are 'cult heroes', and during the Premiership years, Arsenal Football Club has been blessed with a number of them:

CULT HEROES

JOHN JENSEN

'Shoooooooooooooooot!' If you spent any time in North London on Saturday afternoons in the early to mid-1990s, the chances are that you'd have heard this cry from the stands of Highbury.

Having arrived at the Club in the wake of his wonder goal in the 1992 European Championship Final, Jensen took 98 matches to break his duck for The Gunners. The longer the drought lasted, the more fascination surrounded his quest for a goal, prompting Gunners fans to make the aforementioned cry whenever and wherever on the field Jensen got the ball.

The goal finally came on New Year's Eve 1994, and what a wonderful strike it was. There had never been any malice intended in the Arsenal fans' jokes about Jensen's profligacy, and the fact that the Dane clearly enjoyed the fun cemented his cult status.

PERRY GROVES

His best years were behind him when the Premiership era got underway, but Perry Groves was the quintessential cult hero, possessing all the necessary qualities by the bagful.

For a start, Groves was never anything less than supremely committed during his Arsenal career. Even the most demanding of supporters will forgive much in a player as long as they can see him trying and the ginger-haired Groves was always one to try.

Dubbing him Tintin because of his spiky haircut, the fans devoted the song 'We All Live In A Perry Groves World' to him. He borrowed the song's title for his autobiography, which was much like the man himself: honest, entertaining and quirky.

▲ *Danish delight, John Jensen*

GILLES GRIMANDI

Arriving in the summer of 1997 alongside more exotic purchases such as Emmanuel Petit and Marc Overmars, Gilles Grimandi took a little while to win over the Arsenal fans. However, once he did, he enjoyed a very special relationship with them.

At first resembling a gallic Leo Sayer, 'The Grimster' was as honest as they come. He would play wherever he was asked to and would rarely complain when he was not asked to play anywhere. He was not afraid to be physical either and received a number of red cards, including one at the Nou Camp.

In an era when some footballers have become global superstars, Grimandi was very down-to-earth. His eccentric musings on his personal website and honest efforts on the pitch made him a cult hero.

▶ *Fantastic Frenchman, Gilles Grimandi*
▼ *Perry Groves, the man they call Tintin*

THIERRY HENRY

When he signed for the Club Thierry Henry was a World Cup winner. However, so extraordinarily successful was his Arsenal career that his glorious Premiership reign outshone his international achievements in the eyes of most observers.

THIERRY HENRY
(1999/2000–2006/07)
POSITION:
STRIKER
APPEARANCES:
369
GOALS:
226
BORN:
**PARIS, FRANCE,
17 AUGUST 1977**

CLUB HONOURS:
**LEAGUE CHAMPIONSHIP 2002,
2004; FA CUP 2002, 2003**
OTHER HONOURS:
92 FRANCE CAPS (40 GOALS)
OTHER CLUBS:
MONACO, JUVENTUS

Thierry Henry was in so many ways the archetypal Premiership-era Arsenal player. He arrived at the Club needing to prove himself after a difficult spell, as did Bergkamp and Overmars; he was moved to a new position, as were Toure and Petit; and he has electric pace and a sublime first touch, like Wright, Anelka, Walcott and many other Gunners.

Henry's achievements at Arsenal are legendary: he is Arsenal's all-time greatest goal-scorer, and he won two league championships and two FA Cups. He was also been awarded five Player of the Year awards and twice came second in the Fifa World Player of the Year poll while at Arsenal.

Who would have thought that the shy winger who arrived in North London in 1999 could go on to achieve all this? Perhaps only Arsène Wenger – who moved Henry from the wing to centre-forward – could have predicted that his new signing, with his flair, lightning

pace, and eye for goal, could become such a potent force. Such an entertaining one, too: to observe Henry in full-flight is nothing short of the ultimate footballing treat.

Not only did the Arsenal captain score a great many of the goals, he was also a team player who set up a healthy amount of strikes for his team-mates. In 2003–04, he scored 30 goals but set up 20 more as the Gunners won the League Championship without losing a single league game.

Wenger often spoke of the psychological impact that having Henry in the side had on Arsenal's opponents. The manager also ventured that Henry was still to reach his peak, especially following his injuries in the 2006–7 season. Is he Arsenal's greatest ever player? Many Gunners fans would say so. He left the Club for Barcelona in 2007. The love and respect he showed for the fans as he departed was warmly reciprocated.

'HE IS POTENT AND ENTERTAINING: TO OBSERVE HENRY IN FULL-FLIGHT IS NOTHING SHORT OF THE ULTIMATE FOOTBALLING TREAT'

JERMAINE PENNANT

JERMAINE PENNANT
(1999/2000–2004/05)
POSITION:
MIDFIELDER
APPEARANCES:
26
GOALS:
3

BORN:
NOTTINGHAM,
15 JANUARY 1983
OTHER CLUBS:
NOTTS COUNTY, WATFORD,
LEEDS UNITED, BIRMINGHAM CITY,
LIVERPOOL

During his time with Arsenal, Pennant showed flashes of brilliance, and few associated with the Club will be surprised that he has become an important player with a big club.

Since moving to Liverpool, Jermaine Pennant has begun to fulfil the promise that so many saw in him as a teenager. The subject of an attention-grabbing swoop when he was just 15, the former Notts County player arrived in North London with more expectation on his shoulders than most at that age could be expected to carry.

Not that Pennant seemed troubled by the hype; he proved to be a very speedy player with a superb crossing ability. However, the youngster struggled to string many games together. He was loaned to Watford and then returned to score a hat-trick in a 6-1 victory over Southampton. It would be another 48 league matches until Arsenal faced defeat.

By then, Pennant had flown the nest. After spells with Leeds and Birmingham came the move to Liverpool where he has started to show the Premiership what he is capable of.

DAVOR SUKER

DAVOR SUKER
(1999–2000)

POSITION:
STRIKER

APPEARANCES:
39

GOALS:
11

BORN:
OSIJEK, CROATIA,
1 JANUARY 1968

OTHER HONOURS:
2 YUGOSLAVIA CAPS (1 GOAL);
69 CROATIA CAPS (45 GOALS)

OTHER CLUBS:
NK OSIJEK, DINAMO ZAGREB,
SEVILLA, REAL MADRID,
WEST HAM UNITED,
1860 MUNICH

I n summer 1999 Nicolas Anelka left Arsenal, prompting Arsène Wenger to buy two new strikers.

One was Davor Suker, a Croatian goal ace who had scored 110 times in 220 games for Real Madrid and had proved himself in international tournaments. The other was a Frenchman who had also starred on the big stage but was less well-known in England at the time. Given football's ability to surprise, it was the Frenchman, Thierry Henry, who would eclipse the Croatian in the colours of Arsenal.

Sukor scored just 11 goals during his solitary season at Arsenal, but he also only started 15 games, so the goal figure takes on a much more impressive resonance. Among these were two double-goal appearances, against Sunderland and Aston Villa. The latter performance was particularly memorable. The Gunners fell behind in the 44th minute, but a goal either side of half-time from Suker sent them on their way to victory.

The emergence of Thierry Henry and his growing understanding with Dennis Bergkamp kept Suker in the dug-out for much of that campaign. In the summer, he was offered the chance to move to West Ham United, and given his appetite for regular football, the Croatian took the opportunity, but not before he had won the hearts of many at Arsenal.

EDU

To adapt a well-known saying about the city that Arsenal play in: when you tire of Edu, you tire of life – as was made clear when he left the club in 2005.

EDU (EDUARDO CESAR GASPAR)
(2000/01–2004/05)

POSITION:
MIDFIELDER

APPEARANCES:
127

GOALS:
15

BORN:
SAO PAOLO, BRAZIL,
15 MAY 1978

CLUB HONOURS:
LEAGUE CHAMPIONSHIP 2002, 2004; FA CUP 2002, 2003, 2005

OTHER HONOURS:
15 BRAZIL CAPS

OTHER CLUBS:
CORINTHIANS, VALENCIA

The Brazilian was one of those players who, the longer he stayed with the Club, the more affection and respect he earned.

A wholehearted player, Edu had superb all-round abilities. He was a fine passer and crosser of the ball, tackled firmly yet fairly, and also had a fine eye for the goal, particularly in big matches. Nonetheless, it took Edu some time to claim a regular first team place. His patience was rewarded when his time came during the 2001–02 campaign as the Gunners closed in on the Double. The range of Edu's talents was effective and priceless as he could help open up tight games, and then maintain the lead once it was secured.

In subsequent campaigns, Edu scored vital goals away to Manchester United in the FA Cup and to Celta Vigo in the Champions League. His second of two strikes against Celta Vigo was marvellous: he dribbled past three defenders and curled a shot into the top corner. He also netted memorable strikes at Highbury against Blackburn Rovers and Chelsea. The arrival of his fellow countryman Gilberto in the summer of 2002 had made his first-team run-outs more rare, but Edu did not complain.

Rarely has a player left a football club on better terms with the fans than when the smiling Brazilian left Arsenal in the summer of 2005. In his final game at Highbury – the magnificent 7-0 demolition of Everton – Edu was allowed to step up and take a penalty. As he dispatched the ball into the back of the net, the thunderous cheer of the crowd and the visible delight of his team-mates, showed the warmth that was felt for this fantastic player and extraordinary character.

Edu moved from Arsenal to Valencia. Should fate ever dictate that he returns to face Arsenal in the Champions League, he would be guaranteed a warm and rousing reception from the home fans who remember him fondly.

'THE VISIBLE DELIGHT OF HIS TEAM-MATES SHOWED THE WARMTH THAT WAS FELT FOR THIS FANTASTIC PLAYER AND EXTRAORDINARY CHARACTER'

ASHLEY COLE

Ashley Cole transformed himself from a teenage striker with the Arsenal Academy to a world-class left-back. He first joined the Club when he was 12, and by the time he was 19 he was a first team regular and had represented England in the senior side.

ASHLEY COLE
(1999/2000–2005/06)
POSITION:
DEFENDER
APPEARANCES:
228
GOALS:
9
BORN:
STEPNEY, LONDON,
20 DECEMBER 1980

CLUB HONOURS:
LEAGUE CHAMPIONSHIP 2002, 2004; FA CUP 2002, 2003, 2005
OTHER HONOURS:
58 ENGLAND CAPS
OTHER CLUBS:
CRYSTAL PALACE (LOAN), CHELSEA

Enormous natural ability, the close attention of Arsenal coaches throughout his development, and a successful loan spell with Crystal Palace were responsible for the glorious start to Cole's career.

An attacking left-back, Cole built on his early success to cement his place with Club and country. Not only did Cole prevent wingers from mounting profitable attacks, he showed such speed, adventurousness and flair that he often outclassed them at their own game. He was also a tough tackler with a naturally great positional sense.

Many would be overwhelmed at the thought of deposing a Brazilian, but Cole did just that in 2000 when Silvinho was injured. Quickly, he made the position his own, and he went on to form a potent left flank force with Robert Pires

and Thierry Henry. Opposition defenders must have dreaded facing those three.

Although a defender, Cole's Arsenal career is replete with memorable attacking moments, including scoring from a free-kick against Manchester City in October 2000, and his last-gasp winner against Dynamo Kiev in November 2003, which continued Arsenal's involvement in that season's Champions League.

A key contributor to numerous Arsenal successes including the 2002 Double and the 2004 unbeaten season, everything seemed set for Cole to become another long-serving Arsenal left-back in the tradition of Eddie Hapgood, Kenny Sansom and Nigel Winterburn. However, Cole left Arsenal in 2006 and has since become part of the much-respected back-line at Stamford Bridge.

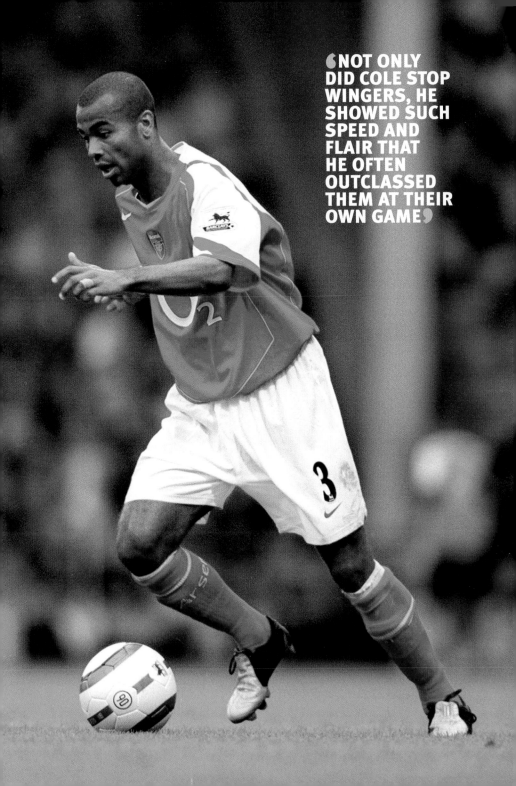

‘NOT ONLY DID COLE STOP WINGERS, HE SHOWED SUCH SPEED AND FLAIR THAT HE OFTEN OUTCLASSED THEM AT THEIR OWN GAME’

GRAHAM BARRETT

RHYS WESTON

GRAHAM BARRETT
(1999/2000–2002/03)
POSITION:
STRIKER
APPEARANCES:
3
BORN:
DUBLIN, IRELAND,
6 OCTOBER 1981

OTHER HONOURS:
6 IRISH CAPS
(2 GOALS)
OTHER CLUBS:
BRISTOL ROVERS,
CREWE ALEXANDRA,
COLCHESTER UNITED,
BRIGHTON, COVENTRY
CITY, SHEFFIELD
WEDNESDAY,
LIVINGSTON, FALKIRK

RHYS WESTON
(1999/2000)
POSITION:
DEFENDER
APPEARANCES:
3
BORN:
KINGSTON-UPON-
THAMES, SURREY,
27 OCTOBER 1980

OTHER HONOURS:
7 WELSH CAPS
OTHER CLUBS:
CARDIFF CITY,
VIKING FK,
PORT VALE

One of Barrett's first-team matches for Arsenal came in the FA Cup tie against Farnborough Town. Arsenal fans, in jovial mood, sang 'We've got Graham Barrett, we've got Graham Barrett' to the youngster. However, his best moment at the Club was winning the 2000 FA Youth Cup.

The tough-tackling defender never managed to repeat his excellent reserve form in the Arsenal first team for which he made just one appearance. After rebuilding his career at Cardiff City, he played in the Norwegian league and has won a number of caps for Wales.

JULIAN
GRAY

BRIAN
MCGOVERN

JULIAN GRAY
(1999/2000)
POSITION:
MIDFIELDER
APPEARANCES:
1

BORN:
LEWISHAM, LONDON,
21 SEPTEMBER 1979
OTHER CLUBS:
CRYSTAL PALACE,
CARDIFF CITY,
BIRMINGHAM CITY

BRIAN MCGOVERN
(1999/2000)
POSITION:
DEFENDER
APPEARANCES:
1
BORN:
DUBLIN, IRELAND,
28 APRIL 1980

OTHER CLUBS:
QUEEN'S PARK
ROVERS, NORWICH
CITY, PETERBOROUGH
UNITED, ST PATRICK'S
ATHLETIC, LONGFORD,
SHAMROCK ROVERS,
BRAY WANDERERS

Some players fail to make it at Arsenal and never really bounce back from the disappointment. Gray, who made his sole first-team appearance against Newcastle in May 2000, has bounced back. After over 100 games for Crystal Palace, the left-sided midfielder now plays for Birmingham City.

Fast and tall, the Irishman could play at centre-back or right-back. However, he failed to make either position his own during his one-game Arsenal first-team career. He has since played for a number of other English clubs including Queens Park Rangers before returning to his native Ireland.

ROBERT PIRES

In May 2002, Pires lifted the Premiership trophy. His team-mates bowed down in front of him, in praise of the fantastic contribution he had made to the double-winning campaign.

ROBERT PIRES
(2000/01–2005/06)
POSITION:
MIDFIELDER
APPEARANCES:
284
GOALS:
84
BORN:
**REIMS, FRANCE,
29 OCTOBER 1973**

CLUB HONOURS:
**LEAGUE CHAMPIONSHIP 2002,
2004; FA CUP 2003, 2005**
OTHER HONOURS:
79 FRANCE CAPS (14 GOALS)
OTHER CLUBS:
METZ, MARSEILLE, VILLARREAL

Robert Pires had been named the PFA's and Football Writers' player of the year; the world was at his feet. Yet, had you encountered the Frenchman in the autumn of 2000, you would never have predicted such a bright future for him.

Pires arrived at Arsenal exhausted from the summer's European Championships and he was daunted by his first glimpse of the combative English Premiership. He wondered how he was going to fit into this league and, in truth, many supporters were asking the same question during his early months at the Club when he appeared nervous and unsettled.

Slowly, though, he made his mark: a stupendous goal against Lazio in the Champions League and a winner in the FA Cup semi-final against Tottenham were a taste of the football to come. However, it was not until 2001–02 that we began to witness the Pires that became a Highbury legend: the swashbuckling, two-footed star who thrilled his supporters with his passing and eye for the goal.

In the Double-winning year of 2002, his interplay with Henry, Ljungberg and Wiltord was heavenly at times. So were some of his goals, including his perfectly executed lob at Aston Villa in March. Weeks later he picked up a cruciate ligament injury that ruled him out until a few months into the following campaign.

However, he came back strongly and scored 14 goals in 26 Premiership appearances in 2002–03. Among these were his three against Southampton in the match that launched the 49-match unbeaten run. He was a star player throughout that historic league sequence and that deserves to be our final memory of him in an Arsenal shirt, rather than his early substitution in the 2006 Champions League Final. He was sacrificed to allow Manuel Almunia to replace the dismissed Jens Lehmann. Pires took this decision professionally but his expression was heartbreaking. A fine player in a fantastic era for the Club, Robert Pires left Arsenal fans with many glorious memories.

'THE SWASHBUCKLING, TWO-FOOTED STAR WHO THRILLED HIS SUPPORTERS WITH HIS PASSING AND EYE FOR THE GOAL'

DAVID
BENTLEY

DAVID BENTLEY
(2002/03–2005/06)
POSITION:
STRIKER
APPEARANCES:
9
GOALS:
1

BORN:
**PETERBOROUGH,
CAMBRIDGESHIRE,
27 AUGUST 1984**
OTHER CLUBS:
**NORWICH CITY,
BLACKBURN ROVERS**

David Bentley was full of confidence and ambition, and had bags of natural talent. Perhaps the only thing he did not have was enough patience to bide his time at Arsenal.

Bentley's first Arsenal goal was a sublime chip against Middlesbrough in an FA Cup fourth round tie. He had come on as a substitute for Dennis Bergkamp, and it was hoped by many supporters that he would eventually replace the Dutchman.

Bentley certainly showed signs of Bergkamp talent and enjoyed playing behind the main strikers where his quick-thinking and deft touches created havoc. However, despite giving him occasional run-outs in all competitions, Arsène Wenger was unable to offer Bentley the amount of action he demanded. A parting of the ways became inevitable. After loan spells with Norwich City and Blackburn Rovers, his move to Ewood Park was made permanent in 2006 and his successful form there has surprised nobody at Arsenal, least of all Wenger who has expressed his pleasure at the progress of his former charge. Notable goals include his 25-yard volley against Salzburg in the Uefa Cup and a hat-trick against Manchester United.

STUART TAYLOR

STUART TAYLOR
(2000/01–2004/05)

POSITION:
GOALKEEPER

APPEARANCES:
30

BORN:
ROMFORD, ESSEX,
28 NOVEMBER 1980

CLUB HONOURS:
LEAGUE CHAMPIONSHIP 2002

OTHER CLUBS:
BRISTOL ROVERS, CRYSTAL
PALACE, PETERBOROUGH UNITED,
LEICESTER CITY (LOAN),
ASTON VILLA

Having impressed in the Arsenal youth ranks and appeared for the England Under-20 team at the 1999 Fifa World Youth Championship, Stuart Taylor was thrown into the deep end in 2001.

During an injury crisis, he was brought on to face Manchester United and Juventus, and the baby-faced giant performed admirably. Against Juventus, he made three fine saves early in the match, without which the Gunners would not have claimed victory.

Thereafter, his chances for first-team action were few and far between. Springy, with good positioning and reactions, he was, thought, a worthy deputy to David Seaman, and played enough games during the 2001–02 season to claim a Premiership medal.

However, once Jens Lehmann and Manuel Almunia arrived, Taylor fell further down the pecking-order, and after a loan spell at Leicester, he moved to the Midlands full-time with Aston Villa. Having played on the highest stage and pocketed a championship medal, Taylor has had to rebuild his career. With his undoubtable talent, he seems set to continue and gain further successes in the future.

SYLVAIN WILTORD

Wiltord arrived at Arsenal having scored a crucial goal in France's victory over Italy in the Final of the 2000 European Championships and with Arsenal's then highest ever transfer fee.

SYLVAIN WILTORD (2000/01–2003/04)	CLUB HONOURS: LEAGUE CHAMPIONSHIP 2002, 2004; FA CUP 2002, 2003
POSITION: STRIKER	OTHER HONOURS: 92 FRANCE CAPS (26 GOALS)
APPEARANCES: 175	OTHER CLUBS: RENNES, BORDEAUX, LYON
GOALS: 49	
BORN: NEUILLY-SUR-MARNE, FRANCE, 10 MAY 1974	

He had also recently finished as the top scorer in the French league. Although Sylvain Wiltord never quite lived up to his advance billing, he was a very successful Arsenal player.

The former Bordeaux striker played well in a number of positions for the Club, including main striker, support striker, and a very effective right-winger. He was fast, had a great pass and shot in his armoury, and rarely seemed to tire or give up. No wonder Wenger had been so tempted by him. It took a short while for Wiltord to settle, but once he did he became an enormously popular figure.

With the Gunners operating on so many fronts, Wiltord was often held back for FA Cup matches and he made many excellent contributions to the Club's progress in the competition, where six of his first 15 goals were scored. However, his most memorable moment for the Club came in the Premiership when he scored the winning goal at Old Trafford in May 2002. He picked up the ball from Barthez's parry and slotted it home with a coolness that belied the magnitude of the occasion and the goal itself. This goal confirmed the Club's third Double and was one of the sweetest moments in Arsenal's history.

Perhaps this moment of glory fired his confidence, as he went on to score six goals in the first six Premiership matches the following season, netting 13 in total during that season. He also claimed his second FA Cup winners' medal with a substitute appearance against Southampton in Cardiff. The unbeaten 2003–04 campaign was, on a personal level, somewhat disappointing for Wiltord due to a lengthy lay-off through injury. However, he made enough appearances to gain a Championship medal and leave the Club on a real high.

HIS GOAL CONFIRMED THE CLUB'S THIRD DOUBLE AND WAS ONE OF THE SWEETEST MOMENTS IN ARSENAL'S HISTORY

RICHARD
WRIGHT

RICHARD WRIGHT (2001/02)	**CLUB HONOURS:** LEAGUE CHAMPIONSHIP 2002
POSITION: **GOALKEEPER**	OTHER HONOURS: **2 ENGLAND CAPS**
APPEARANCES: **22**	OTHER CLUBS: **EVERTON, IPSWICH TOWN**
BORN: **IPSWICH, SUFFOLK, 5 NOVEMBER 1977**	

For six years, Richard Wright had been the unchallenged number one goalkeeper for Ipswich Town, notching up 240 appearances.

When he arrived at Arsenal, his role was to be a very different one – deputizing for, and aiming to replace, the ever-popular David Seaman.

An extremely able all-round talent, Wright's most memorable outings in the 2001–02 season came in the FA Cup. He also made some commendable performances in the Premiership and in European competition. However, in the latter, he conceded a weak shot against Deportivo La Coruna and was ruled out for a period through injury.

Wright will hope to be given another chance to make an impression on the international stage. He has to date won two caps, saving a penalty in his international debut against Malta. First, though, he must establish himself as Ipswich Town's number one, having returned to the club from Everton in 2007.

TOMAS
DANIELEVICIUS

TOMMY
BLACK

RYAN
GARRY

TOMAS DANIELEVICIUS
(2000/01)

POSITION:
STRIKER

APPEARANCES:
3

BORN:
KLAIPEDA, LITHUANIA,
18 JULY 1978

OTHER HONOURS:
17 LITHUANIA CAPS
(10 GOALS)

OTHER CLUBS:
BRUGGE, DYNAMO
MOSCOW, LAUSANNE,
DUNFERMLINE ATHLETIC,
BEVEREN, LIVORNO,
AVELINO, BOLOGNA

TOMMY BLACK
(1999/2000)

POSITION:
MIDFIELDER

APPEARANCES:
2

BORN:
CHIGWELL, ESSEX,
26 NOVEMBER 1979

OTHER CLUBS:
CARLISLE UNITED,
BRISTOL CITY,
CRYSTAL PALACE,
BRADFORD CITY,
SHEFFIELD UNITED,
GILLINGHAM

RYAN GARRY
(2002/03–PRESENT)

POSITION:
DEFENDER

APPEARANCES:
2

BORN:
HORNCHURCH, ESSEX,
29 SEPTEMBER 1983

The striker had to compete for a place against Henry, Kanu, Wiltord and Bergkamp. He was talented, but his performances were never exceptional. His best form has come for his country.

Black was sent out twice on loan before he made his Arsenal debut, and despite showing promise at Highbury, the plucky winger was sold to Crystal Palace where his performances earned him praise.

The nippy defender made his first start in the 6-1 win against Southampton – the first of the 49-match unbeaten league run. However, a shin splint injury sidelined him and checked his progress.

LAUREN

Lauren was like a lion in the Arsenal team – ferocious, formidable and the possessor of incredible nerve. A combative yet cultured talent, like many Wenger signings, he considerably enhanced his reputation while with the Gunners.

LAUREN (LAUREANO BISAN-ETAME MAYER) (2000/01–2006/07)	**BORN:** LONDI KRIBI, CAMEROON, 19 JANUARY 1977
POSITION: DEFENDER	**CLUB HONOURS:** LEAGUE CHAMPIONSHIP 2002, 2004; FA CUP 2002, 2003, 2005
APPEARANCES: 241	**OTHER HONOURS:** 25 CAMEROON CAPS (2 GOALS)
GOALS: 9	**OTHER CLUBS:** UTRERA, SEVILLA, LEVANTE, REAL MALLORCA, PORTSMOUTH

He also acquired a new position. Arriving as a right-sided midfielder in 2000, Lauren showed quickly why Wenger had signed him. A player with an extremely effective touch, he could also close down and challenge opponents. As with so many other players, Wenger decided to switch his positions and tried him as a right-back.

Lauren's transformation from midfield to defence might not be as celebrated as Henry's move from the wing to centre-forward, but it was no less effective. Before Lee Dixon hung up his boots in 2002, the Cameroonian had already proved that he was more than ready to replace him.

In his subsequent four years, he was a rock in the back four. Having destroyed yet another opposition attack, he would surge forward and spark an assault from his own side. He also had considerable confidence as was seen by his cool spot-kicks against Tottenham in the tense run-in to the 2002 title and against Manchester United in the 2005 FA Cup Final. Both penalties were successfully converted.

As the Gunners won the 2004 title without losing a single league match, Lauren was perhaps at his peak. He was named in the PFA Premiership Team of the Year for the season. However, the following campaign saw him suffer a serious injury that kept him out of action for nearly a year.

By the time he returned to fitness, Emmanuel Eboue and Justin Hoyte had both impressed in the right-back slot, and Lauren was allowed to leave the Club. That this lionheart chose Portsmouth as his new employers, when more lucrative but less ambitious opportunities were no doubt on the table, speaks volumes for him. He was reunited with Tony Adams and Sol Campbell at the south-coast club where his performances have been typically wholehearted.

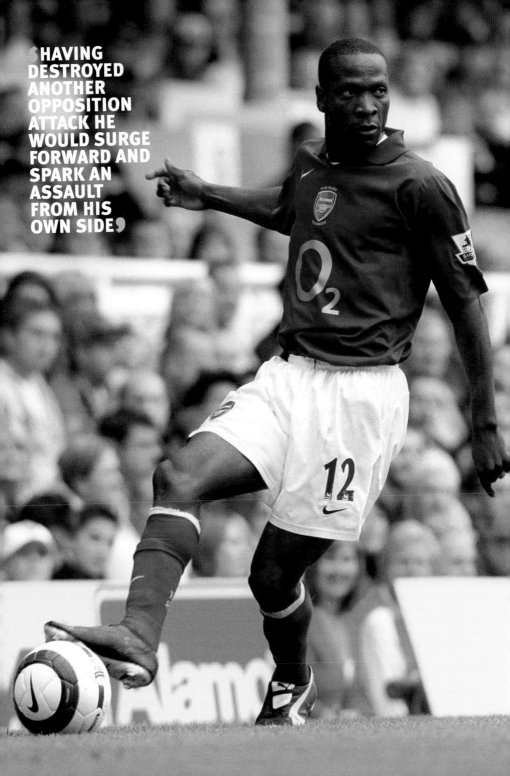

'HAVING DESTROYED ANOTHER OPPOSITION ATTACK HE WOULD SURGE FORWARD AND SPARK AN ASSAULT FROM HIS OWN SIDE'

PLANET ARSENAL

BRAZIL ————————————————
Silvinho
Edu
Gilberto
Julio Baptista
Denilson

ARGENTINA ————————————————
Fabian Cabellero
Nelson Vivas

HOLLAND
Glenn Helder
Dennis Bergkamp
Marc Overmars
Quincy Owusu-Abeyie
Gio van Bronckhorst
Robin van Persie

NORWAY
Pal Lydersen

SWEDEN
Anders Limpar
Stefan Schwarz
Fredrik Ljungberg
Sebastian Larsson
Rami Shaaban

ESTONIA
Mark Poom

SCOTLAND
Paul Dickov
Scott Marshall

DENMARK
John Jensen

LATVIA
Igor Stepanovs

GERMANY
Alberto Mendez
Stefan Malz
Jens Lehmann

LITHUANIA
Thomas Danilevicius

NORTHERN IRELAND
Steve Morrow

BELARUS
Alexander Hleb

WALES
John Hartson
Rhys Weston

CZECH REPUBLIC
Tomas Rosicky

UKRAINE
Oleg Luzhny

IRELAND
David O'Leary
Brian McGovern
Graham Barrett

SWITZERLAND
Johan Djourou
Philippe Senderos

AUSTRIA
Alex Manninger

PORTUGAL
Luis Boa Morte

FRANCE
Remi Garde
Nicolas Anelka
Patrick Vieira
Gilles Grimandi
Emmanuel Petit
David Grondin
Thierry Henry
Robert Pires
Sylvain Wiltord
Jeremie Aliadiere
Pascal Cygan
Gael Clichy
Mathieu Flamini
Abou Diaby
William Gallas

CROATIA
Davor Suker

SPAIN
Cesc Fabregas
Manuel Almunia
Jose Antonio Reyes

ITALY
Arturo
Lupoli

GREECE
Stathis
Tavlaridis

GUINEA
Kaba Diawarra

CAMEROON
Lauren
Alexandre Song

LIBERIA
Christopher Wreh

TOGO
Emmanuel Adebayor

NIGERIA
Nwankwo Kanu

IVORY COAST
Kolo Toure
Emmanuel Eboue

SOL CAMPBELL

What could motivate a man to make the move across North London from Tottenham Hotspur to Arsenal, and switch his loyalties from one bitter rival to another?

SOL CAMPBELL
(2001/02–2005/06)
POSITION:
DEFENDER
APPEARANCES:
197
GOALS:
11
BORN:
PLAISTOW, LONDON,
18 SEPTEMBER 1974

CLUB HONOURS:
LEAGUE CHAMPIONSHIP 2002,
2004; FA CUP 2002
OTHER HONOURS:
69 ENGLAND CAPS (1 GOAL)
OTHER CLUBS:
TOTTENHAM HOTSPUR,
PORTSMOUTH

The answer, in Sol Campbell's case, came at the end of his first season with Arsenal; he won a Premiership winners' medal, to go alongside the FA Cup winners' medal he had won a few days earlier.

Campbell's tall and powerful build belied his intelligent style of play and considered, quiet persona. If you were to list the different qualities that an ideal back four should possess – including strength, tactical awareness, athleticism, pace, and good distribution – all could be found in Campbell alone. This should not surprise: during his schooling at Tottenham Hotspur, he had played in every position except goalkeeper.

Athletic, powerful and determined, Campbell proved a hit for Arsène Wenger's team, which won the Double in the defender's first campaign with the Club. He didn't just marshall the defence with authority, he also scored key goals in both the Premiership and FA Cup campaigns. His choice of Highbury was vindicated. One of his finest performances came against Chelsea on Boxing Day 2001. It was not just his goal – a emphatic header – that impressed. His all-round peformance that day was a key factor in guiding Arsenal to their 2-1 victory.

Inevitably, he faced unpleasant abuse from Tottenham fans but, during his first return to White Hart Lane in November 2001, he appeared to thrive on these outbursts and raised his game accordingly.

A colossus during the 49-match unbeaten run, Campbell complemented the emerging Kolo Toure perfectly, and winning the 2003–04 Premiership title at White Hart Lane must have been sweet for the former Spurs favourite. His final season with the Gunners was a difficult, and at times, disappointing one for Campbell, but it was typical of him to bounce back with a goal in the Champions League Final.

He left for a new challenge with Portsmouth in 2006, where he teamed up once again with his former partner Tony Adams, and quickly became a towering presence for Pompey.

'IF YOU WERE TO LIST THE DIFFERENT QUALITIES THAT AN IDEAL BACK FOUR SHOULD POSSESS, ALL COULD BE FOUND IN CAMPBELL ALONE'

GIOVANNI VAN BRONCKHORST

GIOVANNI VAN BRONCKHORST
(2001/02–2003/04)

POSITION:
MIDFIELDER/DEFENDER

APPEARANCES:
64

GOALS:
2

BORN:
ROTTERDAM, HOLLAND, 5 FEBRUARY 1975

CLUB HONOURS:
**LEAGUE CHAMPIONSHIP 2002
FA CUP 2003**

OTHER HONOURS:
67 HOLLAND CAPS (4 GOALS)

OTHER CLUBS:
RKC WAALWIJK, FEYENOORD, GLASGOW RANGERS, BARCELONA

Like many professionals who play in a number of different positions, Giovanni van Bronckhorst acquitted himself admirably for Arsenal, but rarely hit the headlines.

He was expected to fill the void that had been opened by the departure of Emmanuel Petit, but instead he spent much of the time as wide midfielder or at left back.

A highly intelligent player, van Bronckhorst at full flow gave his team a dependable and adept outlet and the supporters a master class in all-round ability. Quick, neat and determined, the former Rangers man never disappointed whenever he lined up in the starting eleven.

Things were looking good for player and Club until he suffered a cruciate ligament injury that sidelined him until well into his second season. Once back, there was only time and opportunity for him to make 15 league starts, the most memorable of which came against Chelsea in January when he scored a fine goal from 20 yards out.

In the summer of 2003, van Bronckhorst joined Barcelona, where he played under the tutelage of fellow Dutchman Frank Rijkaard.

FRANCIS JEFFERS

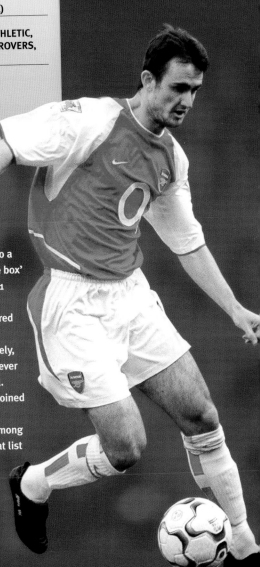

FRANCIS JEFFERS
(2001/02–2003/04)

POSITION:
STRIKER

APPEARANCES:
38

GOALS:
8

BORN:
LIVERPOOL, MERSEYSIDE,
25 JANUARY 1981

OTHER HONOURS:
1 ENGLAND CAP (1 GOAL)

OTHER CLUBS:
EVERTON, CHARLTON ATHLETIC,
RANGERS, BLACKBURN ROVERS,
IPSWICH TOWN

When he signed for Arsenal in June 2001, Francis Jeffers seemed to be the perfect signing.

During the previous month's FA Cup Final, Arsenal had been unable to convert their dominance of the game into a victory, leading Thierry Henry to crave a 'fox in the box' to play alongside him. Could the England Under-21 ace be the answer to Henry's prayers?

Jeffers' abilities were not in doubt; he had starred in a poor Everton side, terrifying opposition defenders with his shrewd movement. Unfortunately, due to considerable bad luck with injury, Jeffers never had a real chance to show his abilities for Arsenal.

Jeffers must have had confidence because he joined a Club that already listed Thierry Henry, Dennis Bergkamp, Sylvain Wiltord and Nwankwo Kanu among its attackers. Forcing his way to the top two of that list was always going to be a challenge, and so it proved for Jeffers, who only made two starts in his first Arsenal season. The following season saw him make 10 starts and score six goals. He returned to Everton the following year.

GILBERTO

For five years, the only constant in Arsenal's central midfield has been the dominant force of Gilberto. The man known in Brazil as the 'invisible wall' is as solid as they come.

GILBERTO (GILBERTO APARECIDO DA SILVA)
(2002/03–PRESENT)

POSITION:
MIDFIELDER

APPEARANCES:
208

GOALS:
23

BORN:
LAGOA DA PRATA, BRAZIL, 7 OCTOBER 1976

CLUB HONOURS:
LEAGUE CHAMPIONSHIP 2004;
FA CUP 2003, 2005

OTHER HONOURS:
47 BRAZIL CAPS (3 GOALS)

OTHER CLUBS:
AMERICA MINIERO, ATLETICO MINEIRO

The Brazilian international arrived at the Club with a World Cup winners' medal in his pocket and he quickly proved his worth on his debut in the 2002 Community Shield when his forward surge ended with him converting a neat cut-back from Dennis Bergkamp. That goal proved to be the winner against Liverpool.

Gilberto established himself quickly as one of the top-flight's most accomplished holding midfielders; he wins tackles, shields the back four, and distributes the ball with assurance and accuracy. He can also score with his head and his foot; a thumping header in the 3-2 defeat of Newcastle United in 2003–04 was particularly memorable.

Gilberto has twice had to soften the blow of Arsenal losing a captain. When Patrick Vieira left the Club in 2005, it was the Brazilian who assumed his pivotal role in the middle of the park. Then, when Thierry Henry was injured for most of the 2006–07 season, Gilberto took the armband and became the driving force of the team. He even made up for some of the goals that Henry would have scored, notching a respectable 11 from midfield that season.

Given his tenure with the Club, it is natural that the powerful midfielder should be looked up to by his youthful team-mates. What a great example he sets: never one to receive or crave the limelight, Gilberto has gone about his work with a consistent and quiet determination. With Henry's move to Barcelona, Gilberto can once again step up to the breach and make his class and composure tell in a young Gunners side.

‘GIVEN HIS TENURE WITH THE CLUB, IT IS NATURAL THAT THE POWERFUL MIDFIELDER SHOULD BE LOOKED UP TO BY HIS YOUTHFUL TEAM-MATES. WHAT A GREAT EXAMPLE HE SETS’

JEREMIE ALIADIERE

JEREMIE ALIADIERE
(2001/02–2006/07)
POSITION:
STRIKER
APPEARANCES:
51
GOALS:
9

BORN:
**RAMBOUILLET, FRANCE,
30 MARCH 1983**
CLUB HONOURS:
LEAGUE CHAMPIONSHIP 2004
OTHER CLUBS:
**CELTIC (LOAN), WEST HAM UNITED
(LOAN), WOLVERHAMPTON
WANDERERS (LOAN),
MIDDLESBROUGH**

During the 2006–07 season, Aliadiere found himself in the peculiar position of being the second-longest serving player in the Arsenal squad and yet having made fewer first-team appearances than many of his team-mates. Behind this anomaly lies a tale of injuries and loan spells.

A product of Clairefontaine's famous National Institut de Football – which also produced Nicolas Anelka and Thierry Henry – Aliadiere made his first-team debut in the Carling Cup in November 2001. However, a hernia complaint in 2002–03 was the first of a number of injuries that blighted his progress. Loan spells at Celtic, West Ham United and Wolverhampton Wanderers followed.

The Frenchman returned to Arsenal for the 2006–07 season and his pace and accurate finishing were in evidence during the Carling Cup campaign. He scored both goals in the 2-0 victory over West Bromwich Albion, then laid on a brace during the 6-3 victory over Liverpool. Against Tottenham in the semi-final second-leg, he clipped home Denilson's cross with the final kick of the first-half of extra-time to turn the tide in Arsenal's favour. It is impossible to imagine anything but further glory for this young man.

In the summer of 2007 he swapped one red shirt for another when he moved to Middlesborough.

PASCAL CYGAN

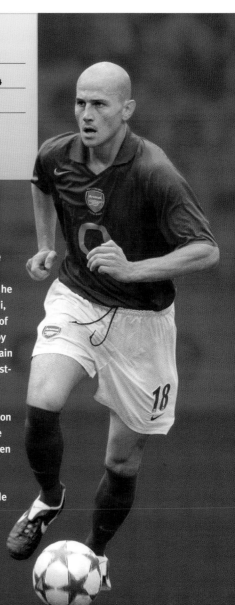

PASCAL CYGAN (2002/03–2005/06)	**BORN:** LENS, FRANCE, 29 APRIL 1974
POSITION: DEFENDER	**OTHER HONOURS:** LEAGUE CHAMPIONSHIP 2004
APPEARANCES: 98	**OTHER CLUBS:** LILLE, VILLARREAL
GOALS: 3	

Pascal Cygan's two goals were vital in beating Fulham in August 2005, as was his assured performance in defence. Yet three years earlier, when Cygan first arrived at the Club, such a positive scenario for him would have seemed unlikely.

When the 6ft 4in defender arrived from Lille in 2002, he was welcomed warmly by former Gunner Gilles Grimandi, whose number 18 shirt Cygan inherited. However, some of his early performances for the Club were characterized by nerves and uncertainty. As the Gunners attempted to retain the Premiership title, the lack of regularity in Cygan's first-team run-outs was perhaps part of the reason for the absence of authority in his play.

His first goal came in a March 2003 victory over Everton (2-1) and it capped perhaps his performance to date. The following season saw a change in fortunes for Cygan when he was allowed a continued run in the team during the winter and produced some fine performances. Over the course of the Championship-winning season, Cygan made a significant contribution to the unbeaten campaign.

In 2005–06, up against the fine form of Kolo Toure, Cygan had to wait for his chances. He joined Villarreal in the summer of 2006.

For as long as football is discussed, the achievements of Arsenal's 49-match unbeaten run will be remembered. Between 7 May 2003 and 16 October 2004 they were simply invincible in the league and collected a Premiership title during the unbeaten run. Here are the vital statistics for the Gunners heroes who made the most appearances:

THE INVINCIBLES!

THIERRY HENRY

RUN HISTORY:
48 GAMES (4,312 MINUTES)

KEY INVINCIBLE MOMENT:
ARSENAL 4 LIVERPOOL 2 (9 APRIL 2004)

Having recently exited both the FA Cup and the Champions League, the Gunners found themselves trailing 2-1 at half-time against Liverpool. The title charge and unbeaten run both seemed in jeopardy. Within five minutes of the restart, they were ahead thanks to Henry who first set up Pires to score, and then powered through the Liverpool defence to score himself. Who would have thought he was carrying a back injury?

KOLO TOURE

RUN HISTORY:
48 GAMES (4,174 MINUTES)

KEY INVINCIBLE MOMENT:
ARSENAL 2 BOLTON WANDERERS 2 (18 SEPTEMBER 2004)

A tied game that Arsenal could have lost so easily. One of the most dangerous moments came in the first half when Jens Lehmann dropped a long throw by Jay-Jay Okocha and Kolo Toure was forced to make a desperate clearance just in front of the goal line.

▲ *Thierry Henry, Arsenal V Liverpool, 9 April 2004*

JENS LEHMANN

RUN HISTORY:
47 GAMES (4,230 MINUTES)

KEY INVINCIBLE MOMENT:
NEWCASTLE UNITED 0 ARSENAL 0 (11 APRIL 2004)

During the first half of this tie Alan Shearer crossed from the right and Craig Bellamy's flick deflected off Kolo Toure. The German deftly switched direction and sprawled at full-length to prevent the goal.

ASHLEY COLE

RUN HISTORY
41 GAMES (3,652 MINUTES)

KEY INVINCIBLE MOMENT:
MANCHESTER CITY 0 ARSENAL 1
(25 SEPTEMBER 2004)

In the 14th minute of this game, Jose Antonio Reyes attempted to pass to Cole. Although Richard Dunne intervened, the ball ended up with Cole and the defender coolly slotted home. Between this goal and the clean-sheet he helped keep at the other end, the defender was a key man in the 47th match of the unbeaten run.

ROBERT PIRES

RUN HISTORY
45 GAMES (3,432 MINUTES)

KEY INVINCIBLE MOMENT:
SOUTHAMPTON 0 ARSENAL 1 (29 DECEMBER 2003)

Earlier in the year, Robert Pires had scored the only goal of the game as Arsenal beat the Saints to win the FA Cup. He repeated the trick here in the Premiership after some fine interplay between Dennis Bergkamp and Thierry Henry. His goal earned a vital three points.

▲ *Robert Pires, Southampton away, 29 December 2004*
◄ *Kolo Toure, Arsenal V Bolton, 18 September 2004*

KOLO TOURE

At the start of the 2003–04 season, Arsène Wenger moved Kolo Toure to a new position. Within 10 months, the Ivorian had a nomination for the PFA Young Player Of The Year and a Premiership medal to his name.

KOLO TOURE
(2002/03–PRESENT)
POSITION:
DEFENDER
APPEARANCES:
244
GOALS:
11
BORN:
SOKOURA BOUAKE,
IVORY COAST,
19 MARCH 1981

CLUB HONOURS:
LEAGUE CHAMPIONSHIP 2004;
FA CUP 2005
OTHER HONOURS:
45 IVORY COAST CAPS (2 GOALS)
OTHER CLUBS:
ASEC ABIDJAN

This was by no means the first time that Wenger had reinvented a player to great effect; both Emmanuel Petit and Thierry Henry were moved to new positions. Toure's move was just as successful a transformation. He turned out to be a natural centre-back: strong and fast, he times his tackles to perfection, and has superb positioning and tactical awareness.

Not that Toure's first season should be ignored. In his first league appearance Toure scored an equalizing header at Chelsea and was named Man of the Match. However, it was the unbeaten league campaign of 2003–04 that saw Toure become a firm favourite: he missed just one league match as the Gunners made history with that magnificent sequence.

Although not a prolific goal-scorer, Toure hit the target when it mattered during the Champions League semi-final first-leg against Villarreal. He burst into the box in the 41st minute and converted Alexander Hleb's pass. The following campaign saw him score four times, including a low volley at White Hart Lane.

During his time with Arsenal, Toure has become an influential figure to his younger team-mates. With his wholehearted, determined approach and his leadership skills, this tremendous professional may be captaincy material in the future. Although not a product of the Arsenal Academy, he is almost regarded to be by his fans, such has been his meteoric rise at the Club.

'WITH HIS WHOLEHEARTED, DETERMINED APPROACH AND HIS LEADERSHIP SKILLS, THIS TREMENDOUS PROFESSIONAL MAY BE CAPTAINCY MATERIAL'

STATHIS
TAVLARIDIS

RAMI
SHAABAN

STATHIS TAVLARIDIS
(2001/02–2003/04)

POSITION:
DEFENDER

APPEARANCES:
8

BORN:
SERRRES, GREECE,
25 JANUARY 1980

OTHER HONOURS:
2 GREECE CAPS

OTHER CLUBS:
ELPIDA PROVATA,
IRAKLIS,
PORTSMOUTH,
LILLE

RAMI SHAABAN
2002/03–2003/04

POSITION:
GOALKEEPER

APPEARANCES:
5

BORN:
STOCKHOLM,
SWEDEN,
30 JUNE 1975

OTHER HONOURS:
11 SWEDEN CAPS

OTHER CLUBS:
SALTSJÖBADENS IK,
AL-ZAMALEK,
DJUREARDENS IF,
ITTIHAD OSMAN,
NACKA FF,
DJURGÅRDEN,
VÄRTANS IK,
BRIGHTON & HOVE
ALBION, FREDRIKSTAD

Versatile Tavlaridis played at both centre-back and right-back for the Gunners. He made a good start, his debut coming in the 4-0 League Cup victory over Manchester United in November 2001. However, he failed to impose himself consistently on matches, and was loaned to Portsmouth briefly before being sold to the French side Lille.

Shaaban's two years with Arsenal were plagued by injuries. The goalkeeper suffered a broken leg among other ailments and was limited to just five appearances for the first team. Among them was one against PSV in the Champions League in November 2002. He had little to do but managed a clean sheet.

KERREA
GILBERT

QUINCY
OWUSU-ABEYIE

KERREA GILBERT
2005/06–PRESENT

POSITION:
DEFENDER

APPEARANCES:
9

BORN:
HAMMERSMITH,
LONDON,
28 FEBRUARY 1987

OTHER CLUBS:
CARDIFF CITY

**QUINCY OWUSU-
ABEYIE**
2003/04–2005/06

POSITION:
STRIKER

APPEARANCES:
23

GOALS:
2

BORN:
AMSTERDAM,
HOLLAND,
15 APRIL 1986

OTHER CLUBS:
SPARTAK MOSCOW

'I like Kerrea because he is a winner and a fighter', said Arsène Wenger of his London-born defender. The right-back is full of strength and pace and has appeared for the Gunners in all four competitions. He was loaned to Cardiff City for the 2006–07 season where he impressed observers.

Owusu-Abeyie is a product of the famed Ajax youth system. The striker once scored six goals in one match for the Arsenal Under-17s, but his achievements for the Club's first team were more modest. The Dutchman left the Club in 2006 for Spartak Moscow.

GAEL CLICHY

GAEL CLICHY
(2003/04–PRESENT)
POSITION:
DEFENDER
APPEARANCES:
97

BORN:
TOULOUSE, FRANCE,
26 JULY 1985
CLUB HONOURS:
LEAGUE CHAMPIONSHIP 2004
OTHER CLUBS:
CANNES

Having been Ashley Cole's understudy, when the England left-back departed the Club, Gael Clichy was thrust into first-team reckoning. Given the assured way that he goes about his work, it was no surprise that he was undaunted by succeeding Cole.

Nor that the former Cannes left-back made such a success of it, for the Frenchman has much in common with his predecessor: he is a sharp, effective defender with fine pace and overlapping skills. In the 2007 Carling Cup semi-final second-leg victory against Tottenham, it was a characteristic forward surge by Clichy which led to Emmanuel Adebayor's opener.

His form during the 2006–07 campaign earned him his first international call-up for France which capped his return from the stress fracture injury he sustained while playing for the French under-21s. He also earned renewed respect of the Arsenal fans who had first taken him to their hearts as he became the youngest Gunner to win a Premiership medal in 2004.

Having starred all season, Clichy ended the 2006–07 campaign vowing to improve in the future. World-class performers in sport never rest on their laurels – Clichy could soon be joining that elite.

PHILIPPE SENDEROS

PHILIPPE SENDEROS (2003/04–PRESENT)	BORN: GENEVA, SWITZERLAND, 14 FEBRUARY 1985
POSITION: DEFENDER	
APPEARANCES: 83	CLUB HONOURS: FA CUP 2005
GOALS: 2	OTHER HONOURS: 15 SWITZERLAND CAPS (3 GOALS)
	OTHER CLUBS: SERVETTE

The number six shirt has a certain aura around it. A strong tackler, powerful in the air and with natural leadership qualities, Phillipe Senderos is often reminiscent of Tony Adams, who wore the same number.

Senderos did not make his first-team debut until over a year after he signed for the Club but his performances during the 2004–05 season were impressive. He was confident in the FA Cup Final against Manchester United where the Gunners kept a clean sheet despite their opponents' rampant mood.

The following campaign began shakily for Senderos, particularly when Chelsea's Didier Drogba outwitted him during a tense derby. However, the youngster bounced back and was a regular member of the defence that amassed a record ten clean sheets in the Champions League – although he missed out on a Champions League Final place through injury. He then starred for Switzerland in the World Cup Finals.

Just as Senderos was gathering some real momentum in his career, injury intervened and blighted his 2006–07 campaign. However, he is a solid character and is likely to be back stronger than ever in the forthcoming season.

JENS LEHMANN

When Jens Lehmann saved Juan Roman Riquelme's last-minute penalty in the 2006 Champions League semi-final, he crystallized his stature as a big-match hero.

JENS LEHMANN
(2003/04–PRESENT)
POSITION:
GOALKEEPER
APPEARANCES:
186
BORN:
ESSEN, GERMANY,
10 NOVEMBER 1969

CLUB HONOURS:
LEAGUE CHAMPIONSHIP 2004;
FA CUP 2005
OTHER HONOURS:
44 GERMAN CAPS
OTHER CLUBS:
SCHALKE, MILAN, BORUSSIA
DORTMUND

For 10 successive games in the competition, the Arsenal's goal had been impenetrable. Lehmann stood guard for seven of these ties as the Gunners marched towards their first final. Illustrious opposition including Juventus and Real Madrid had failed to beat him and with the Gunners 60 seconds from the final, Lehmann was not about to let Riquelme stop their progress so he palmed away the spot-kick.

This performance capped a fine season for the German international. He had produced breathtaking saves throughout 2005–06 including a hat-trick of wonder stops at Anfield. The best of the night came when Philippe Senderos's deflection looked set to cross the line until Lehmann thrust out a hand to stop it. Against Real Madrid, he was astounding when he pawed aside the ball after Raul's shot had hit the post.

Not that his heroics throughout the 2005–06 season came as a huge surprise. It

was Lehmann who kept goal for virtually the whole 49-game unbeaten league run and it was Lehmann who guided the Gunners through the 2005 FA Cup Final against Manchester United, including the penalty shoot-out. From his first season with the Club, Lehmann's experience, shot-stopping ability and safe handling reassured the defence in front of him. This has been essential to the progress of a relatively inexperienced and often very young back four.

David Seaman's legendary Arsenal career will never be forgotten, but it is to the German's immense credit that he has never been compared unfavourably with his predecessor. Goalkeepers are all too easily awarded the status of eccentrics and Lehmann has an entertaining personality. This experienced man has an enormously positive influence on his younger team-mates. He can also continue to have an incredibly positive influence on Arsenal's scorelines, of course.

'THIS
EXPERIENCED
MAN ALSO
HAS AN
ENORMOUSLY
POSITIVE
INFLUENCE
ON HIS
YOUNGER
TEAM-MATES'

JOHAN DJOUROU

JOHAN DJOUROU
(2003/04–PRESENT)
POSITION:
DEFENDER
APPEARANCES:
45
GOALS:
1

BORN:
ABIDJAN, IVORY COAST,
18 JANUARY 1987
OTHER HONOURS:
5 SWITZERLAND CAPS
OTHER CLUBS:
NONE

Djourou had to wait over two years for his Premiership debut, but when he finally made his entrance, it was in a 7-0 victory over Middlesbrough. Looking back at that extraordinary game, Johan Djourou insists that he never let the victory go to his head.

Born in Africa and raised in Geneva, Djourou was a teenager when he moved to Arsenal in 2003. He made his debut the following year in the Carling Cup. Following the victory over Middlesbrough, he had good outings in the Premiership and Champions League.

A fantastic reader of the game, the Swiss international is also fast and assured in possession. His versatility adds to his appeal and he has appeared in both full-back positions as well as his preferred centre-back berth. In 2006–07, injuries to his fellow countryman Phillipe Senderos and William Gallas gave Djourou a chance to stake a claim for a regular first-team spot.

Arsène Wenger has predicted that Senderos and Djourou will be Switzerland's centre-back duo for years to come. They may regularly join forces for the Gunners too.

MATHIEU FLAMINI

MATHIEU FLAMINI
(2004/05–PRESENT)
POSITION:
MIDFIELDER
APPEARANCES:
113
GOALS:
5

BORN:
**MARSEILLE, FRANCE,
7 MARCH 1984**
OTHER CLUBS:
MARSEILLE

In his first season in English football, Mathieu Flamini was an effective, versatile and hard-working midfielder, with an industrious and wholehearted approach to the game, at times reminiscent of Ray Parlour. During the following campaign Wenger was short of a left-back due to injuries, so Flamini took his versatility to a new level and proved to be ideal cover.

The Frenchman nullified a series of right-sided midfielders during the record 10 consecutive clean-sheets the Gunners recorded en route to the 2006 Champions League Final. Perhaps his finest performances came against Real Madrid where he gave David Beckham two of the most frustrating nights of his career with masterful defensive displays. But Mathieu was not stranger to the European stage, having played in a UEFA Cup Final with Marseille.

Flamini was unable to impose himself in the first-team in 2006–07. However, the Frenchman has a big heart and he will surely never be far from first-team football, especially given his professional approach to the game.

FRANCESC FABREGAS

When Cesc Fabregas hit the opener against Juventus in the 2005–06 Champions League campaign, it not only confirmed his maturity but also underlined a changing of the guards in the Arsenal midfield.

CESC FABREGAS (2003/04–PRESENT)	BORN: ARENYS DE MAR, SPAIN, 4 MAY 1987
POSITION: MIDFIELDER	CLUB HONOURS: FA CUP 2005
APPEARANCES: 152	OTHER HONOURS: 16 SPAIN CAPS
GOALS: 13	OTHER CLUBS: NONE

The Spaniard's opposite number for Juventus was Patrick Vieira, his former midfield partner with the Gunners. Fabregas had paid due praise to the Frenchman in the build-up to the tie and then paid his mentor a compliment of sorts by outplaying him on the night. Many were full of praise for the teenager but the Highbury faithful had long been aware of his brilliance.

Making his debut in October 2003 in the Carling Cup, Fabregas became the youngest-ever Arsenal player and then the youngest Arsenal goal-scorer. He hinted at future brilliance from the start and following Vieira's departure, Cesc became the mainstay of the Arsenal midfiled. Technically brilliant, he quickly belied his youth by dictating the pace and rhythm of Arsenal's attacks.

He excels at laying on accurate assists for the strikers, and Fabregas can score himself too. His finish against Juventus stands out, but so does his birthday goal against Liverpool in May 2005, when he jumped onto a Bergkamp pass and rattled the ball past Jerzy Dudek.

Fabregas was a pivotal figure during the latter stages of the 49-match unbeaten run and his form since then has made him an influential presence in the youthful Arsenal side. During the 2006–07 season he notched up 13 assists, which was just one fewer than double Player of the Year Cristiano Ronaldo managed.

During the same campaign, Fabregas went from being the promising youngster who amazed onlookers with his ability and confidence to becoming a star from whom brilliance is now expected. Given not just the excellence of his team-mates and manager, but also his own, determined and focused nature, Fabregas could become the greatest midfielder in the world.

'FABREGAS COULD BECOME THE GREATEST PLAYER IN HIS POSITION IN THE WORLD'

SEBASTIAN
LARSSON

ARTURO
LUPOLI

SEBASTIAN LARSSON (2004/05–2006/07)
POSITION: MIDFIELDER
APPEARANCES: 12
BORN: ESKILSTUNA, SWEDEN, 6 JUNE 1985
OTHER CLUBS: BIRMINGHAM CITY

ARTURO LUPOLI (2004/05–2006/07)
POSITION: STRIKER
APPEARANCES: 9
GOALS: 3
BORN: BRESCIA, ITALY, 24 JUNE 1987
OTHER CLUBS: PARMA, DERBY COUNTY, FIORENTINA

An accurate player, Larsson appeared in all four competitions during his Arsenal career. His best moments came in the Carling Cup where he set up a goal for Robin van Persie at Sunderland and scored in a penalty shoot-out at Doncaster. After a loan spell at Birmingham City, he secured a permanent move there in January 2007.

With 17 goals in 15 games for the reserves in 2005–06, there was no doubt that Lupoli was deadly in front of goal. However, his first-team chances for Arsenal were limited, though he memorably scored twice against Everton in the Carling Cup. It was during a loan spell at Derby County that he agreed a five-year deal with Fiorentina.

MANUEL ALMUNIA

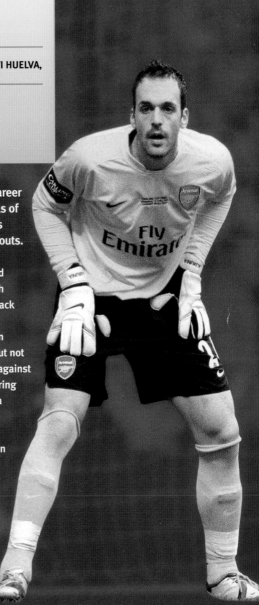

MANUEL ALMUNIA
(2004/05–PRESENT)
POSITION:
GOALKEEPER
APPEARANCES:
43

BORN:
**PAMPLONA, SPAIN,
19 MAY 1977**
OTHER CLUBS:
**CE SABADELL, RECREATIVI HUELVA,
CELTA VIGO, ALBACETE**

Manuel Almunia has enjoyed an eventful career in North London. He appeared in the finals of the Champions League and Carling Cup, and has guided the Gunners through two penalty shoot-outs. Not bad for an 'understudy'.

An accomplished shot-stopper, the agile Spaniard is also a good handler of the ball and deals well with crosses. If he can improve communication with his back four, he will be an even greater prospect.

Understudies sometimes suffer from nerves when they are thrust into the spotlight of the first-team, but not Almunia. He calmly prevailed in penalty shoot-outs against Doncaster and Sheffield United and was assured during the 2006 Champions League Final against Barcelona when the Gunners were reduced to ten men.

The competition for the first-team goalkeeper position is always very keen, but given his dedication and ability, Almunia will continue to keep his fellow Arsenal custodians on their toes. He also has strong aspirations to participate on the international stage and has hinted that if he is not selected for Spain, then he would be happy to explore the possibility of representing England.

THE HOME BOYS

Throughout the Premiership years, a healthy succession of players have come through Arsenal's youth ranks to star for the Club.

At the start of the Premiership era, the Arsenal team included a number of home-grown players, including Tony Adams, Paul Merson and Paul Davis. All three had graduated from the youth team side, and went on to win two league championships (1989 and 1991). In 1993, they were rejoined by Martin Keown who had left Highbury after coming through the Arsenal youth ranks. Along with Adams, Keown went on to win a number of Premiership titles at Arsenal, starting in 1998.

Another Arsenal player to win a Premiership medal that year was Stephen Hughes. In 1994, Hughes had been in the exciting side as Arsenal won the FA Youth Cup. Other FA Youth Cup winners to make the Arsenal first team in the Premiership era include Neil Heaney and Matthew Rose.

▲ *Paul Merson (1986/87–1996/97)*
◀ *Tony Adams (1983/84–2001/02)*

Arsenal was one of the first English clubs to gain academy status. Since 1998, the Arsenal Academy has regularly produced footballers ready for first-team action. The Academy Director is Arsenal legend Liam Brady. His staff includes two other former Gunners, David Court and Steve Bould. They help develop boys between the ages of nine and 21.

The first, and to date most celebrated, graduate of the Arsenal Academy is Ashley Cole, who has been cited by many as the greatest player in his position in the world. Cole won two Premiership titles with Arsenal. Academy graduates Stuart Taylor and Jeremie Aliadiere also placed Premiership medals on their sideboards in 2002 and 2004 respectively. Meanwhile, the likes of David Bentley and Jermaine Pennant are currently star players with Blackburn Rovers and Liverpool.

The League Cup has proved to be a superb testing ground for Academy graduates and in the 2005–06 season, a team rich with Brady's boys came very close to a place in the Final. Johan

▲ Arsenal Youth Players celebrating winning the Youth Cup (12 May 1994)

▼ Justin Hoyte (V Charlton Athletic, 2 January 2007)

Djourou, Fabrice Muamba, Sebastian Larsson, Arturo Lupoli and Nicklas Bendtner gained valuable experience during that campaign.

However, in season 2006–07, the young Gunners went one better and reached the Final of the Carling Cup. Along the way they beat Liverpool 6-3 at Anfield and saw off local rivals Tottenham Hotspur in a memorable two-legged semi-final.

JUSTIN HOYTE

JUSTIN HOYTE
(2001/02–PRESENT)

POSITION:
DEFENDER

APPEARANCES:
53

GOALS:
1

BORN:
**WALTHAM FOREST, LONDON,
20 NOVEMBER 1984**

OTHER CLUBS:
SUNDERLAND (LOAN)

When he made his unremarkable first-team debut as a last-minute substitute against Southampton in May 2003, none would have predicted that Justin Hoyte was entering football history. However, that was the first match of the 49-game unbeaten league run that put the Club in the history books.

When the magical run was over, the Londoner began to amass settled league runs in the first team. He was loaned to Sunderland for the 2005–06 season and his pacey, adventurous style of play won him many admirers. Against Newcastle United, Hoyte began a move at the back and bombed forward to finish it with his first career goal.

Back in North London the following season, he took the left-back role recently vacated by Ashley Cole and then moved to right-back to cover for the injured Emmanuel Eboue. Against Charlton Athletic, he became the first Englishman to score for Arsenal at Emirates Stadium when he side-footed Henry's pass past Scott Carson. Given the relish with which Hoyte bombs forward, this could be the first of many goals for him.

JOSE ANTONIO REYES

JOSE ANTONIO REYES
(2003/04–PRESENT)

POSITION:
STRIKER

APPEARANCES:
110

GOALS:
23

BORN:
UTRERA, SPAIN,
1 SEPTEMBER 1983

HONOURS:
LEAGUE CHAMPIONSHIP 2004,
FA CUP 2005

OTHER HONOURS:
21 SPAIN CAPS (4 GOALS)

OTHER CLUBS:
SEVILLE, REAL MADRID (LOAN)

Although not a household name when he arrived in England in January 2004, Reyes was considered by seasoned observers to be one of the finest prospects in European football.

Just 20 years old, he had been coveted for some time by Arsène Wenger. This was reflected in the fact that he was the subject of the Club's record transfer fee. However, he had a hellish start when he scored an own goal that helped dump the Gunners out of the Carling Cup.

How quickly could he make amends? In his second month with the Club, he scored twice in five minutes during the fifth round of the FA Cup to knock bitter rivals Chelsea out of the competition. His opener was particularly stunning: cutting in from the right he fired an unstoppable shot from 25 yards out.

Reyes was a star during the second half of the 49-match run, but after being on the receiving end of some heavy treatment at Old Trafford as the sequence ended, he seemed to lose confidence and his previously ever-present smile became a rare sight. Following a year on loan at Real Madrid, he chose to rebuild his career at Atletico Madrid.

ROBIN VAN PERSIE

Robin van Persie says that one of the things he loves about football is that you can 'practise and practise then see the results in a game'. To observe the results of the Dutchman's practice is a joy.

ROBIN VAN PERSIE (2004/05–PRESENT)	**BORN:** ROTTERDAM, HOLLAND, 6 AUGUST 1983
POSITION: STRIKER	**CLUB HONOURS:** FA CUP 2005
APPEARANCES: 110	**OTHER HONOURS:** 19 HOLLAND CAPS (7 GOAL)
GOALS: 34	**OTHER CLUBS:** FEYENOORD

Every Arsenal supporter has their favourite Robin van Persie moment: the choices often include his fearsome volleyed winner at Charlton Athletic in September 2006, or his curled shot from a seemingly impossible angle at home to Blackburn in November 2005, or his arching free-kick against Wigan in the Carling Cup in January 2006.

Given the majesty of these wonder goals, the Rotterdam-born striker has often been compared with Dennis Bergkamp. However, van Persie wants to be assessed in his own right as was seen by his refusal to consider inheriting Bergkamp's number 10 shirt on his departure from the Club. On his arrival at Highbury in August 2004 it was not just his fellow Dutchman that van Persie looked to for motivation, but Robert Pires. He says that watching the French winger made him up his game by 10 per cent.

Van Persie went on to terrorize defences with his quick feet and even quicker mind. In his first season in England he scored twice in the FA Cup semi-final against Blackburn Rovers to send the Gunners to Cardiff. The way he turned Lucas Neill for the first goal was typical of the way he torments defenders.

The Dutchman's importance to the Club was underlined in the 2006–07 season when a broken metatarsal ended his campaign prematurely in January. He had already scored 13 goals at that stage and his absence cast a shadow over the rest of the season. However, van Persie is an explosive force and so his frustration at being on the sidelines may only add to his potency in front of goal.

‘GIVEN THE MAJESTY OF THESE WONDER GOALS, THE ROTTERDAM-BORN STRIKER HAS OFTEN BEEN COMPARED WITH DENNIS BERGKAMP’

EMMANUEL ADEBAYOR

As a child, Adebayor watched Arsenal matches on television and was enthralled by the form of his hero Nwankwo Kanu. Nowadays, he plays for Arsenal and is often compared to his former football idol.

EMMANUEL ADEBAYOR (2005/06–PRESENT)	BORN: LOME, TOGO, 26 FEBRUARY 1984
POSITION: STRIKER	OTHER HONOURS: 37 TOGO CAPS (16 GOALS)
APPEARANCES: 57	OTHER CLUBS: METZ, MONACO
GOALS: 16	

When Adebayor signed for the Gunners he said that he likes 'treating the ball as though it is something special' and he also promised to repay the confidence that Arsenal showed in him with goals. He has kept to his word on both counts. Netting with a close-range header on his debut against Birmingham City, he scored 12 goals in 32 starts in his first full season with Arsenal.

The striker says that it was the quick passing style of the Gunners that encouraged him to sign for the Club and he has indeed slotted perfectly into this style of play. Although his height, strength and pace are major strong points, Manu shows true grace on the ball. He has elements of Kanu's unpredictability, but is a much faster and more consistent performer than his childhood hero. On the pitch he is a player to be considered in his own right, regardless of who his heroes are.

Perhaps Adebayor's most heroic performance came at Old Trafford in September 2006. Deployed as the lone frontman, the Togo international worked tirelessly all afternoon, then held off the attentions of Wes Brown to hit a richly deserved winner in the 86th minute.

At the age of 20, Adebayor appeared in a Champions League Final with Monaco, and his goals were crucial to Togo's successful qualification campaign for the 2006 World Cup, where he appeared in each of his country's group matches. He has shown he can star in the Premiership for the Gunners, but we can also expect big things in European competition too.

With the departure of Thierry Henry the Togan lost a team-mate, but gained the chance to bid for star billing upfront. Given his great ability to hold the ball up, challenge defenders in the air and his increased confidence in front of goal, he has plenty in his favour.

'ALTHOUGH HIS HEIGHT, STRENGTH AND PACE ARE MAJOR STRONG POINTS, MANU SHOWS TRUE GRACE ON THE BALL'

EMMANUEL EBOUE

EMMANUEL EBOUE	**BORN:**
(2004/05–PRESENT)	ABIDJAN, IVORY COAST,
POSITION:	4 JUNE 1983
DEFENDER	**OTHER HONOURS:**
APPEARANCES:	14 IVORY COAST CAPS
71	**OTHER CLUBS:**
GOALS:	BEVEREN
2	

For any young player to be compared to the legendary, multi-World Cup winning Brazilian winger Garrincha would be a proud moment. When that young player is a defender, the praise takes on an even keener edge.

When Emmanuel Eboue was compared to the Brazilian by Wenger, he had just spent the duration of Arsenal's 5-0 victory over Aston Villa in April 2006 bombing up and down the flank. The Ivorian has lived up to Wenger's praise and has created a right-flank understanding with Alexander Hleb not unlike the old left-back partnership enjoyed by Ashley Cole and Robert Pires.

Eboue also has defensive strength, as Real Madrid's Robinho would testify, after the Champions League clash at the Bernabéu in 2006. A determined and competitive character, Eboue has gone from strength to strength since he arrived in North London in 2005. He can also score goals, as he did with a fantastic long-range shot against Sunderland in the Carling Cup. Having signed a long-term contract with Arsenal, Eboue shows every sign of becoming a fixture in the back four for many years to come.

ALEXANDER HLEB

ALEXANDER HLEB (2005/06–PRESENT)	**BORN:** MINSK, BELARUS, 1 MAY 1981
POSITION: **MIDFIELDER**	OTHER HONOURS: **27 BELARUS CAPS (4 GOALS)**
APPEARANCES: **88**	OTHER CLUBS: **BATE BORISOV, VFB STUTTGART**
GOALS: **6**	

As a child, Alexander Hleb played football on concrete pitches in Belarus. However, despite his boyhood hard-knock matches, it still took him a while to adjust to the rigours of English football. Despite starting his Arsenal career promisingly, an injury picked up on international duty ruled him out for over a month and it took him a while to return to that level of fitness.

When he scored in the 7-0 demolition of Middlesbrough in January 2006, everything clicked into place. This was followed by a cracking performance reminiscent of his play-making days in the German league followed by Real Madrid in the Champions League. In a comfortable 3-0 defeat of Charlton Athletic, Hleb pulled the strings for the strikers and then surged forward to finish from 12 yards.

The Belarussian has a superb understanding with Emmanuel Eboue on the right flank. He also zig-zags across the playing surface and therefore creates an air of unpredictability for opponents. Effective with both feet he reads the game well and has old-fashioned dribbling skills. With his difficult start a distant memory, Hleb is now very much at home in the Premiership.

TOMAS ROSICKY

TOMAS ROSICKY
(2006/07–PRESENT)

POSITION:
MIDFIELDER

APPEARANCES:
37

GOALS:
6

BORN:
PRAGUE, CZECH REPUBLIC,
4 OCTOBER 1980

OTHER HONOURS:
62 CZECH REPUBLIC CAPS
(22 GOALS)

OTHER CLUBS:
SPARTA PRAGUE, BORUSSIA
DORTMUND

Tomas Rosicky signed to the club just prior to the 2006 World Cup, so Arsenal fans found themselves watching the Czech Republic's matches with a keen interest. They liked what they saw: his two goals against USA stood out, including a long volley.

The Czech didn't reproduce that goalscoring form every week in the Premiership but this lively midfielder has nonetheless been a colossal performer for the Gunners. Fast and highly skilled, the former star of the Bundesliga is an accurate and intelligent passer of the ball. He is also a great finisher, as was seen when he headed home against Wigan in February 2007, a performance that helped earn him the arsenal.com Player of the Month Award.

By the age of 25, Rosicky had already represented his nation in three tournaments, won league titles in the Czech Republic and Germany, and amassed 31 appearances in the Champions League. Given his own abilities and those of his Arsenal team-mates, the best times could be yet to come for the man who orchestrates play so well that he has become known as 'the little Mozart'.

ABOU
DIABY

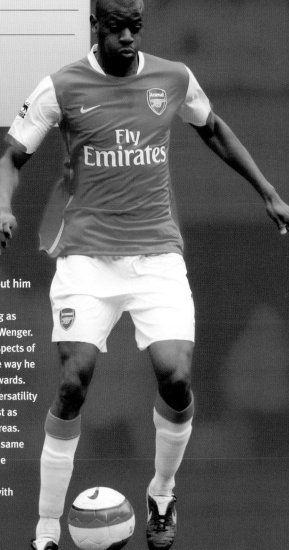

ABOU DIABY
(2005/06–PRESENT)

POSITION:
MIDFIELDER

APPEARANCES:
34

GOALS:
2

BORN:
PARIS, FRANCE,
11 MAY 1986

OTHER CLUBS:
AUXERRE

rsenal's first signing of the
January 2006 transfer window,
Abou Diaby settled in quickly. Tall,
strong and courageous, he was an
incredible addition to the Arsenal
midfield. However, an ill-timed
challenge during the 3-0 win
against Sunderland in May 2006
fractured and dislocated his ankle and put him
out of action for eight months.

He returned from injury at least as strong as
before – even stronger according to Arsène Wenger.
The manager also agreed that Diaby has 'aspects of
Patrick Vieira in his game', most notably the way he
shrugs off challenges and marshals the forwards.
However, he is his own man and has more versatility
than Vieira, as is seen when he performs just as
well on the wing as he does in the central areas.

This young man progressed through the same
Auxerre youth academy as Eric Cantona. If he
continues to apply himself with the level of
dedication he has shown so far, his career with
Arsenal could be hugely fruitful.

THEO WALCOTT

Walcott had been billed as a potential 'wonder boy' of English football and had already proved his pedigree prior to signing with the Gunners in 2006.

THEO WALCOTT (2005/06–PRESENT)	BORN: STANMORE, LONDON, 16 MARCH, 1989
POSITION: STRIKER	OTHER HONOURS: 1 ENGLAND CAP
APPEARANCES: 32	OTHER CLUBS: SOUTHAMPTON
GOALS: 1	

Before he made a first-team appearance for Arsenal, Theo Walcott had already represented England at under-16s and under-17s level, been a non-participating member of the senior side at the 2006 World Cup Finals, and been nominated for the BBC Young Sports Personality of the Year award. As a result, Gunners fans were full of anticipation as to what the former Southampton player could do in a red shirt.

Walcott showed enormous maturity and poise in his early performances for Arsenal, setting up Gilberto's goal on his debut against Aston Villa, thus claiming the first assist at Emirates Stadium. Confident and focused, he is very fast both with and without the ball at his feet. He is also an accomplished finisher as he showed during his early games for the Saints, including a brilliantly measured lob from outside the area against Luton.

The 2004 FA Youth Cup-winner's first goal in an Arsenal shirt came in the Carling Cup Final against Chelsea and what a cracker it was. Collecting a poorly cleared corner, Walcott passed to Diaby who returned the ball. He curled it past Petr Cech. The sheer joy of his memorable aeroplane celebration was widely shared. People have told the polite, affable Walcott that they have never been happier to see someone break their duck.

He says he chose Arsenal because he wanted to learn from Arsène Wenger and play alongside his hero Thierry Henry. With his ability, dedication and mature personality, Walcott himself is a shining example to any aspiring footballer.

'HE SHOWED ENORMOUS MATURITY AND POISE IN HIS EARLY PERFORMANCES FOR ARSENAL. CONFIDENT AND FOCUSED, HE IS VERY FAST BOTH WITH AND WITHOUT THE BALL AT HIS FEET'

WILLIAM GALLAS

Gallas was by no means a typical Wenger signing. He was approaching his 30s, very much the finished article, and with extensive experience of the English Premiership.

WILLIAM GALLAS (2006/07–PRESENT)	BORN: ASNIÈRES-SUR-SEINE, FRANCE, 17 AUGUST 1977
POSITION: DEFENDER	OTHER HONOURS: 52 FRANCE CAPS (2 GOALS)
APPEARANCES: 29	OTHER CLUBS: CAEN, MARSEILLE, CHELSEA
GOALS: 3	

Having won two league championships and a League Cup at Stamford Bridge, it is not difficult to see why the Manager made a move for him. Strong and fast with an incredible spring, he was a rock in an excellent defensive Chelsea side.

The French international quickly became a hit with the Arsenal faithful. A series of commanding displays in defence were capped with some incisive attacking play, including some memorable goals. His first came against Sheffield United in September: following some fine play from his fellow countryman Thierry Henry – with whom he shares a birthday – he lashed a fantastic volley high into the net. He also nodded home against Liverpool two months later.

Gallas often mentions his desire to test himself by finding new challenges. It was such a quest that brought him to England and then made him move across London. Such an attitude will always be welcome among the fans, displaying as it does a hunger that is not always found in players of Gallas' age.

During an interview Gallas also once reflected: 'I'm no Pele, Maradona or Zidane, but I know I am hard-working and mentally strong'. This is very true and it is highly doubtful that any of those three players would have relished the challenge of playing against William Gallas. Neither would any Premiership centre-forward relish this challenge; and Gallas looks set to keep the backline clean for the Gunners for years to come.

'HE OFTEN MENTIONS HIS DESIRE TO TEST HIMSELF BY FINDING NEW CHALLENGES. IT WAS SUCH A QUEST THAT BROUGHT HIM TO ENGLAND AND THEN MADE HIM MOVE ACROSS LONDON

One of the most exciting times for any football fan is watching a hot-shot prospect take his place in the team for the first time. It is the thought that this youthful prospect could go on to become a star and give those watching the chance to say, 'I was there for his debut'. Arsenal's history is packed with teenage idols like John Radford, Ray Kennedy, Paul Vaessen, Liam Brady, Paul Merson and Tony Adams. During the Premiership years plenty of players have made their first team debut before the age of 20. Here is a selection:

TEEN SPIRIT

RAY PARLOUR

PREMIERSHIP DEBUT:
LIVERPOOL 2 ARSENAL 0 (29 JANUARY 1992)

Ray Parlour's Premiership debut at the age of 18 years was the stuff of nightmares: he conceded a penalty which contributed to Arsenal's 2-0 defeat at Anfield. However, his third league start came at the same ground and this time he provided the assist for both goals in a 2-0 victory, making him a hit with the fans. By the end of his first full season he had collected winners' medals in both the FA Cup and League Cup after the youngster starred in both visits to Wembley to face Sheffield Wednesday.

JOHN HARTSON

PREMIERSHIP DEBUT:
ARSENAL 1 EVERTON 1 (14 JANUARY 1995)

Hartson became the most expensive teenager in British football when he joined the Club in as a 19-year-old in January 1995. The Gunners faithful warmed to him quickly for his passion and power. After a respectable debut, he scored in his second match for Arsenal away to Coventry City, and hit the target again in his next tie at home to Southampton.

NICOLAS ANELKA

PREMIERSHIP DEBUT:
CHELSEA 0 ARSENAL 3 (5 APRIL 1997)

Anelka's debut when he was 18 years old came as a substitute with just six minutes left of a London derby at Stamford Bridge. His next three appearances came as a substitute and his somewhat nervous performances gave little indication that, by the end of his first full season with the Gunners, Nicolas would be a star of the double-winning campaign.

MATTHEW UPSON

PREMIERSHIP DEBUT:
COVENTRY CITY 2 ARSENAL 2 (17 JANUARY 1998)

Upson, as an 18-year-old, was the first English player bought by Arsène Wenger at Arsenal, having made just one league outing for Luton Town before he became a Gunner. He got his first Premiership chance thanks to an injury to Marc Overmars, which forced Wenger to shuffle the pack and bring Upson into defence alongside Steve Bould. Despite the disappointing scoreline, his debut was impressive and assured.

ASHLEY COLE

PREMIERSHIP DEBUT:

NEWCASTLE UNITED 4 ARSENAL 2 (14 MAY 2000)

Ashley was first recruited by Arsenal at the
tender age of 12 and was held in special
affection by the fans from the start. He was
19 years old when he was picked for his first
Premiership game because Wenger was resting
the big guns ahead of the following week's
Uefa Cup Final. Cole fared better in his second
Premiership game when he scored the
equalizer at Bradford City.

▲ *The first teenage idol to score at Emirates Stadium
was Theo Walcott against Aston Villa*

GAEL CLICHY

PREMIERSHIP DEBUT:

ARSENAL 3 BIRMINGHAM CITY 0 (22 NOVEMBER 2003)

With Martin Keown, Lauren, Ray Parlour and
Patrick Vieira unavailable through suspension
and Gilberto and Sylvain Wiltord missing due
to international duty, Wenger threw the 18-year-
old Clichy into midfield for this tie. The press
heaped praise on him. One reporter dubbed
him 'a French Ashley Cole'. Clichy didn't have
to wait long for further Premiership outings.

THEO WALCOTT

PREMIERSHIP DEBUT:

ARSENAL 1 ASTON VILLA 1 (19 AUGUST 2006)

When Walcott took to the field in the 73rd
minute of his first Premiership match at the
tender age of 17 years, the Gunners were facing
the prospect of defeat in their first match at
Emirates Stadium. However, just 11 minutes
into his debut he sent in a cross that Gilberto
converted to equalize. Setting up the Stadium's
first Premiership goal – debuts don't get much
more dramatic than that!

CESC FABREGAS

PREMIERSHIP DEBUT:

EVERTON 1 ARSENAL 4 (15 AUGUST 2004)

With Patrick Vieira injured, the young Spaniard
made his first Premiership appearance during
the tail-end of the historic 49-match unbeaten
run. He showed his class from the start and
became a firm favourite with the fans despite
his tender years. 'He's only 17, he's better than
Roy Keane', they sang. The song continues to
be apt as Cesc shows all the signs of becoming
just as accomplished a player as Keane.

DENILSON

PREMIERSHIP DEBUT:

SHEFFIELD UNITED 1 ARSENAL 0
(30 DECEMBER 2006)

Replacing Tomas Rosicky in the 82nd minute,
there was little that the 18-year-old boy could
do to prevent Arsenal losing this tie. Within
days he was the subject of another 82nd
minute Premiership substitution, replacing
Cesc Fabregas as the Gunners romped to a 4-0
victory against Charlton Athletic. Although only
a substitute, his potential could not be doubted.

JULIO
BAPTISTA

MART
POOM

JULIO BAPTISTA
(2006/07–PRESENT)

POSITION:
MIDFIELDER/STRIKER

APPEARANCES:
25

GOALS:
10

BORN:
SAO PAULO, BRAZIL,
1 OCTOBER 1981

OTHER HONOURS:
20 BRAZIL CAPS

OTHER CLUBS:
SAO PAULO,
SEVILLA,
REAL MADRID

MART POOM
(2005/06–2006/07)

POSITION:
GOALKEEPER

APPEARANCES:
2

BORN:
TALLINN, ESTONIA,
3 FEBRUARY 1972

OTHER HONOURS:
112 ESTONIA CAPS

OTHER CLUBS:
KUPS,
FLORA TALLINN,
PORTSMOUTH,
DERBY COUNTY,
SUNDERLAND,
WATFORD

Arriving from Real Madrid on loan in August 2006, 'The Beast' had been coveted by Arsène Wenger after scoring 38 goals in 63 appearances for Sevilla. He scored four goals at Anfield in the Carling Cup and then enjoyed a prolonged run in the Arsenal first team due to injuries to Thierry Henry and Robin van Persie.

Poom had to wait until the final day of his second season as a Gunner to make his Premiership debut and he kept a clean sheet in the 0-0 draw at Portsmouth. The agile stopper has over 100 international caps and has been voted Estonian Footballer of the Year six times. He has now signed for Watford in the hope of securing regular first team football.

ALEXANDRE SONG

DENILSON

ALEXANDRE SONG
(2005/06–PRESENT)

POSITION:
MIDFIELDER

APPEARANCES:
15

GOALS:
1

BORN:
**DOUALA, CAMEROON,
9 SEPTEMBER 1987**

OTHER CLUBS:
**BASTIA, CHARLTON
ATHLETIC (LOAN)**

DENILSON
(2006/07–PRESENT)

POSITION:
MIDFIELDER

APPEARANCES:
19

BORN:
**SAO PAULO, BRAZIL,
16 FEBRUARY 1988**

OTHER CLUBS:
SAO PAULO

Much-coveted Song joined the Gunners on loan and then signed a permanent deal in June 2006. He was on the scoresheet in the 6-3 Carling Cup victory over Liverpool. Within weeks the tough prospect moved to Charlton Athletic on loan for the remainder of the campaign. A versatile player, Song can operate effectively in defence or midfield.

In his first season in English football Denilson quickly won admirers. He played in a variety of roles in the midfield and his style of play was compared to his team-mate Cesc Fabregas. He has captained the Brazilian Under-20 side and is set for a bright future at club and international level.

GEORGE GRAHAM

Just as he collected many trophies during his reign – six in eight years – so did George Graham gather respect during his time in the Highbury hot seat.

MANAGER:
1986–1995

BORN:
BARGEDDIE, LANARKSHIRE, 30 NOVEMBER 1944

CLUB HONOURS:
LEAGUE CHAMPIONSHIP 1989, 1991; FA CUP 1993; LEAGUE CUP 1987, 1993; EUROPEAN CUP WINNERS' CUP 1994

MANAGERIAL CAREER:
MILLWALL, ARSENAL, LEEDS UNITED, TOTTENHAM HOTSPUR

One of the Club's most successful managers, Graham was always more keen on the idea of respect than the idea of affection. However, his rigid rules and the disciplined style of his teams led to results.

George Graham started as a player for Arsenal, where he helped to win the Double in 1971. He returned to Arsenal in 1986 with a vastly different reputation. Then, he had been known as 'the Stroller' for his laid-back style of play, but having guided Millwall up the Football League, he returned to Highbury with a reputation as a disciplined, hard-working manager with great things ahead of him.

Graham won the League Cup in his first season and then created the greatest period of success the Club had enjoyed since Herbert Chapman's 1930s reign.

A shrewd operator in the transfer market, the likes of Steve Bould, Lee Dixon and Brian Marwood were particularly good-value purchases. He added some fine youth team graduates such as Tony Adams and David Rocastle, and the occasional expensive purchase like David Seaman and Anders Limpar to create the nucleus of the squads that won league championships in 1989 and 1991.

By the time England's top-flight became known as the Premiership, Graham had enjoyed his best days as an Arsenal manager in the league. From then on, his successes came in knock-out competitions, and he was the first manager to guide his side to victories in both the FA Cup and League Cup in the same campaign. His shrewd acquisition Ian Wright was, by now, a goal-scoring phenomenon, but it was Alan Smith's goal that landed the European Cup Winners' Cup in 1994 and gave Graham his best night since his side won the league at Anfield in 1989.

The European victory proved to be Graham's final glory with the Club and he left Highbury the following year. Ultimately, however, Graham will always be remembered for the years of success he brought to Arsenal Football Club during an extraordinary reign.

‘HE WON THE
LEAGUE CUP
IN HIS FIRST
SEASON, THEN
CREATED THE
GREATEST
PERIOD OF
SUCCESS THE
CLUB HAD
ENJOYED SINCE
THE 1930s’

BRUCE RIOCH

Arsenal have had some testing experiences at the hands of Bolton Wanderers, but they had better times under the management of former Bolton manager Bruce Rioch.

MANAGER:
1995/96

BORN:
ALDERSHOT, HAMPSHIRE, 6 SEPTEMBER 1947

MANAGERIAL CAREER:
TORQUAY UNITED, FC SEATTLE, MIDDLESBROUGH, MILLWALL, BOLTON WANDERERS, ARSENAL, NORWICH CITY, WIGAN ATHLETIC, ODENSE BK

In 1994, following a 2-2 draw at Burnden Park in the FA Cup fourth round, Arsenal were beaten 3-1 by Bolton in the Highbury replay. Bruce Rioch's Bolton Wanderers were athletic and easy-on-the-eye that night. The following year, Rioch was the Arsenal manager.

In truth, Arsenal had been anything but easy-on-the-eye during the latter stages of George Graham's reign, so Gunner fans were excited by the prospect of what changes Rioch might bring. The excitement was fuelled further when the new manager quickly unveiled Dennis Bergkamp and David Platt.

It took a while for Rioch's flowing style of football to take shape, not least because Dennis Bergkamp, David Platt and Paul Merson were all players at their deadliest in 'the hole' behind the main attacker. The cliché 'two's company, three's a crowd' proved to be true. However, within a few months, the team were zipping the ball round with aplomb and Highbury was alive with optimism.

But in the second half of the season, clouds began to gather over Rioch. There were reports of a feud between him and some of the more senior players. Ian Wright went as far as handing in a transfer request, which, though it was turned down, hinted at problems in the dressing room. It was also believed that the new manager was unhappy with the Club's new procedures for purchases of players.

This was all far from ideal, but Rioch continued, and led the team to a Top Five Premiership finish, as well as a League Cup semi-final. Though Arsenal lost to Aston Villa, they were at least guaranteed European football for the following season. But Rioch would play no part, as his employment was terminated on the eve of the 1996–97 season. The philosophies of George Graham and Arsène Wenger were so radically different that perhaps Rioch's greatest achievement as manager at Arsenal was as a bridge between the two tenures.

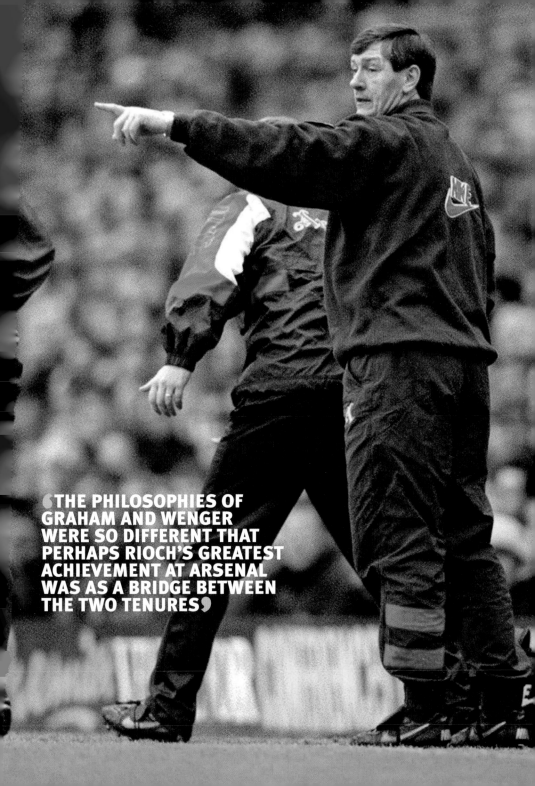

‘THE PHILOSOPHIES OF
GRAHAM AND WENGER
WERE SO DIFFERENT THAT
PERHAPS RIOCH'S GREATEST
ACHIEVEMENT AT ARSENAL
WAS AS A BRIDGE BETWEEN
THE TWO TENURES’

STEWART HOUSTON

ACTING MANAGER
1995 & 1996
BORN:
DUNOON,
SCOTLAND,
20 AUGUST
1949

MANAGERIAL CAREER:
ARSENAL,
QUEEN'S PARK RANGERS

Twice the Acting Manager at Arsenal, Stewart Houston managed during his first temporary spell to achieve a pair of feats unparalleled in the Club's illustrious history.

He guided the team away from the reaches of the relegation zone while steering them to the Final of a major European competition. Houston had taken temporary hold of the reigns following George Graham's exit in February 1995 and immediately rolled his sleeves up and got on with the task in hand. The Club had been shaken by the headline-grabbing departure of Graham and Houston's hand in steadying the nerves should not be underestimated. The team enjoyed three high-scoring victories to move them away from the unfamiliar lower reaches of the table.

Meanwhile, The Gunners swept aside Auxerre and Sampdoria to reach their second successive European Cup Winners' Cup Final. Nayim's party-pooping goal must not detract from Houston's achievement in getting the team to Paris.

A fresh start was needed so the affable Scot was overlooked in favour of Bruce Rioch.

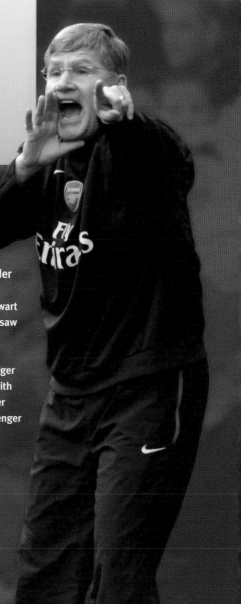

PAT RICE

ACTING MANAGER
1996

BORN:
BELFAST,
NORTHERN IRELAND,
17 MARCH, 1949

A lthough the former Arsenal captain was only Acting Manager for a short time in September 1996, he can take enormous pride in being the only manager with a 100 per cent league record, his teams having won all three Premiership games played under his management.

Stepping up to the role between the departure of Stewart Houston and the arrival of Arsène Wenger, Rice also oversaw the second leg of the UEFA Cup tie against Borussia Moenchengladbach.

Rice neither expected nor wished to receive the manager job full time, but applied himself to the temporary role with characteristic passion and professionalism. When Wenger arrived, Rice's loyalty to the Club was rewarded when Wenger appointed him assistant manager.

ARSÈNE WENGER

The successes of Arsenal's Premiership era have arrived mainly under Arsène Wenger's tenure. Although largely unknown in the UK when he arrived at Arsenal in September 1996, Wenger quickly won respect.

ARSÈNE WENGER
(1996/97–PRESENT)
BORN:
STRASBOURG, FRANCE,
22 OCTOBER 1949
CLUB HONOURS:
LEAGUE CHAMPIONSHIP
1998, 2002, 2004; FA CUP
1998, 2002, 2003, 2005

MANAGERIAL CAREER:
NANCY, AS MONACO, GRAMPUS
EIGHT NAGOYA, ARSENAL

Wenger was the first Frenchman to take control of an English club. One of his first signings, Patrick Vieira, was an instant hit and the introduction of different training methods and diets gave players like Tony Adams and Steve Bould a new lease of life.

He introduced new players including Marc Overmars and Emmanuel Petit and won the Double in 1997–98 – his first full season in the game. He took the Club close to repeating that feat the following year. Opposition fans – who had not long before habitually taunted the Gunners with chants of 'boring, boring Arsenal' – have on occasions clapped Wenger's teams off the field.

A new-look Arsenal team then took shape with Thierry Henry, Freddie Ljungberg, Robert Pires and Sol Campbell joining Bergkamp to play even more stylish football. This team landed Wenger his second Double in 2001–02. Then came the majestic unbeaten league campaign of 2003–04 when Wenger guaranteed himself a permanent place in the record books.

Perhaps most admirably, Wenger has achieved his success without spending big in the transfer market. Wenger's encyclopaedic knowledge of football around the world means he can find a Kolo Toure or a Cesc Fabregas and turn them into big money stars after their signature, rather than prior to it. His knowledge is consistently profitable.

The Club's state-of-the-art modern training centre and new home at Emirates Stadium are both Wenger-influenced innovations. His vision and ambition are all-encompassing and rivalled in the Club's history only by the great Herbert Chapman. The young Arsenal squad of today is also living testament to Wenger's reach: the Club now has a virtual conveyor belt of young men who play the fast, fluid passing-style he so adores.

'Arsène who?' asked the newspapers when he was appointed Gunners manager. Rarely can a question have been answered to such dazzling effect.

'HIS VISION AND AMBITION ARE ALL-ENCOMPASSING AND RIVALLED IN THE CLUB'S HISTORY ONLY BY THE GREAT HERBERT CHAPMAN'

During Arsenal's illustrious and successful recent history, a number of records have been set. Winning sequences, scoring sprees, goal-fest games, points tallies and so much more, here is your guide to the Gunners' greatest moments and achievements during the Premiership era:

CLUB RECORDS

SEQUENCES

CONSECUTIVE PREMIERSHIP WINS:
14 FROM 10 FEBRUARY 2002 (EVERTON 0 ARSENAL 1) UNTIL 18 AUGUST 2002 (ARSENAL 2 BIRMINGHAM CITY 0)

CONSECUTIVE PREMIERSHIP DRAWS:
5 DRAWS FROM 3 JANUARY 1994 (ARSENAL 0 QPR 0) UNTIL 19 FEBRUARY 1994 (EVERTON 1 ARSENAL 1)

CONSECUTIVE PREMIERSHIP MATCHES UNBEATEN:
49 GAMES FROM 7 MAY 2003 (ARSENAL 6 SOUTHAMPTON 1) UNTIL 16 OCTOBER 2004 (ARSENAL 3 ASTON VILLA 1)

CONSECUTIVE PREMIERSHIP HOME MATCHES UNBEATEN:
32 FROM 7 MAY 2003 (ARSENAL 6 SOUTHAMPTON 1) TO 23 JANUARY 2005 (ARSENAL 1 NEWCASTLE UNITED 0)

SCORELINES

BIGGEST HOME WIN IN PREMIERSHIP
ARSENAL 7 EVERTON 0 (12 MAY 2005)
ARSENAL 7 MIDDLESBROUGH 0
(14 JANUARY 2006)

BIGGEST AWAY WIN IN PREMIERSHIP
MIDDLESBROUGH 1 ARSENAL 6 (24 APRIL 1999)

HIGHEST-SCORING HOME DRAW IN THE PREMIERSHIP
ARSENAL 3 CHELSEA 3 (4 SEPTEMBER 1996)
ARSENAL 3 SHEFFIELD WEDNESDAY 3 (9 MAY 2000)
ARSENAL 3 BLACKBURN ROVERS 3
(20 OCTOBER 2001)

HIGHEST-SCORING AWAY DRAW IN THE PREMIERSHIP
LEICESTER CITY 3 ARSENAL 3 (27 AUGUST 1997)

▲ *Patrick Vieira lifting the Commemorative Trophy for the 49 unbeaten run*

PLAYER RECORDS

YOUNGEST PREMIERSHIP APPEARANCE-MAKER
CESC FABREGAS, AGED 17 YEARS 103 DAYS
EVERTON 1 ARSENAL 4 (15 AUG 2004)

OLDEST PREMIERSHIP APPEARANCE-MAKER
JOHN LUKIC, AGED 39 YEARS 336 DAYS
ARSENAL 0 DERBY COUNTY 0 (11 NOV 2000)

YOUNGEST PREMIERSHIP GOAL-SCORER
CESC FABREGAS, AGED 17 YEARS 113 DAYS
ARSENAL 3 BLACKBURN ROVERS 0 (25 AUG 2004)

MOST PREMIERSHIP APPEARANCES
RAY PARLOUR, 333 APPEARANCES

MOST PREMIERSHIP GOALS
THIERRY HENRY, 174 GOALS

MOST PREMIERSHIP GOALS IN A SEASON
THIERRY HENRY, 30 GOALS (2003–04)

▲ *Jermaine Pennant and Robert Pires celebrating*
during the Arsenal V Southampton game, 7 May 2003

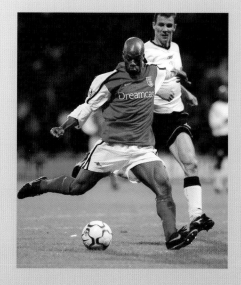

▲ *Sylvain Wiltord scoring the second goal during the*
Bolton Wanderers V Arsenal game, 29 April 2002

MISCELLANEOUS

HIGHEST PREMIERSHIP HOME ATTENDANCE
60,023. ARSENAL 1 ASTON VILLA 1
(19 AUGUST 2006)

LOWEST PREMIERSHIP HOME ATTENDANCE
18,253. ARSENAL 0 WIMBLEDON 1
(10 FEBRUARY 1993)

HIGHEST POINTS TALLY
90 POINTS IN THE 2003–04 SEASON

CUP VICTORIES
THE FIRST CLUB TO WIN BOTH DOMESTIC CUPS
IN THE 1992–93 SEASON

FA CUP HISTORY
IN 2003 ARSENAL RETAINED THE FA CUP FOR THE
FIRST TIME IN ITS HISTORY

PLAYER STATISTICS

This is the record of Arsenal appearances and goals in Premiership matches, covering all players who have played for the Club in Premier League matches since the competition began on 15 August 1992. The dates shown indicate the first year of each season.

PLAYER	SEASONS	APPEARANCES	GOALS
RAY PARLOUR	1991/92–2003/04	333	21
DAVID SEAMAN	1990/91–2002/03	325	0
DENNIS BERGKAMP	1995/96–2005/06	315	87
MARTIN KEOWN	1985/86 & 1992/93–2003/04	310	4
LEE DIXON	1987/88–2001/02	305	10
PATRICK VIEIRA	1996/97–2004/05	279	29
NIGEL WINTERBURN	1987/88–1999/2000	270	4
TONY ADAMS	1983/84–2001/02	255	12
THIERRY HENRY	1999/2000–2006/07	254	174
FREDRIK LJUNGBERG	1998/99–PRESENT	216	46
IAN WRIGHT	1991/92–1997/98	191	104
ROBERT PIRES	2000/01–2005/06	189	62
STEVE BOULD	1988/89–1998/99	175	2
KOLO TOURE	2002/03–PRESENT	166	6
PAUL MERSON	1986/87–1996/97	160	28
LAUREN	2000/01–2006/07	159	6
ASHLEY COLE	1999/2000–2005/06	156	8
GILBERTO	2002/03–PRESENT	147	16
JENS LEHMANN	2003/04–PRESENT	140	0
SOL CAMPBELL	2001/02–2005/06	135	8
NWANKWO KANU	1998/99–2003/04	119	30
GILLES GRIMANDI	1997/98–2001/02	114	4
SYLVAIN WILTORD	2000/01–2003/04	106	31
FRANCESC FABREGAS	2003/04–PRESENT	106	7
MARC OVERMARS	1997/98–1999/2000	100	25
JOHN JENSEN	1992/93–1995/96	98	1
KEVIN CAMPBELL	1987/88–1994/95	97	22
ANDY LINIGHAN	1990/91–1996/97	91	5
DAVID PLATT	1995/96–1997/98	88	13
EMMANUEL PETIT	1997/98–1999/2000	85	9
EDU	2000/01–2004/05	79	7
ALAN SMITH	1987/88–1994/95	75	8
OLEG LUZHNY	1999/2000–2002/03	75	0
MATHIEU FLAMINI	2004/05–PRESENT	72	4
ROBIN VAN PERSIE	2004/05–PRESENT	72	21
JOSE ANTONIO REYES	2003/04–PRESENT	69	16
NICOLAS ANELKA	1996/97–1998/99	65	23
PASCAL CYGAN	2002/03–2005/06	63	3
DAVID HILLIER	1990/91–1996/97	61	1

PLAYER	SEASONS	APPEARANCES	GOALS
GAEL CLICHY	2003/04–PRESENT	61	0
STEVE MORROW	1991/92–1996/97	60	1
ALEXANDER HLEB	2005/06–PRESENT	58	5
SILVINHO	1999/2000–2000/01	55	3
JOHN HARTSON	1994/95–1996/97	53	14
STEPHEN HUGHES	1994/95–1999/2000	49	4
PHILIPPE SENDEROS	2004/05–PRESENT	47	2
EMMANUEL EBOUE	2004/05–PRESENT	43	0
EMMANUEL ADEBAYOR	2005/06–PRESENT	42	12
IAN SELLEY	1992/93–1996/97	41	0
GIOVANNI VAN BRONCKHORST	2001/02–2003/04	41	2
NELSON VIVAS	1998/99–2000/01	40	0
GLENN HELDER	1994/95–1996/97	39	1
ALEX MANNINGER	1997/98–2001/02	39	0
EDDIE MCGOLDRICK	1993/94–1995/96	38	0
STEFAN SCHWARZ	1994/95	34	2
MATTHEW UPSON	1997/98–2002/03	34	0
ANDERS LIMPAR	1990/91–1993/94	33	2
PAUL DAVIS	1979/80–1994/95	32	1
REMI GARDE	1996/97–1998/99	31	0
JEREMIE ALIADIERE	1999/2000–2006/07	29	1
JUSTIN HOYTE	2002/03–PRESENT	29	0
CHRISTOPHER WREH	1997/98–2000/01	28	3
JOHAN DJOUROU	2004/05–PRESENT	28	0
TOMAS ROSICKY	2006/07–PRESENT	26	3
LUIS BOA MORTE	1997/98–1999/2000	25	0
SCOTT MARSHALL	1992/93–1997/98	24	1
ABOU DIABY	2005/06–PRESENT	24	2
JULIO BAPTISTA	2006/07	24	3
FRANCIS JEFFERS	2001/02–2003/04	22	4
PAUL DICKOV	1992/93–1996/97	21	3
WILLIAM GALLAS	2006/07–PRESENT	21	3
DAVOR SUKER	1999/2000	20	8
JIMMY CARTER	1991/92–1994/95	19	2
JOHN LUKIC	1983/84–1989/90 & 1996/97–2000/01	18	0
STUART TAYLOR	2000/01–2004/05	18	0
IGORS STEPANOVS	2000/01–2003/04	17	0
MARK FLATTS	1992/93–1994/95	16	0
THEO WALCOTT	2006/07–PRESENT	16	0

PLAYER STATISTICS

PLAYER	SEASONS	APPEARANCES	GOALS
CHRIS KIWOMYA	1994/95–1997/98	14	3
PAUL SHAW	1994/95–1996/97	12	1
JERMAINE PENNANT	1999/2000–2004/05	12	3
RICHARD WRIGHT	2001/02	12	0
DAVID O'LEARY	1975/76–1992/93	11	0
VINCE BARTRAM	1994/95–1996/97	11	0
MANUEL ALMUNIA	2004/05–PRESENT	11	0
DENILSON	2006/07–PRESENT	10	0
PAL LYDERSEN	1991/92–1992/93	8	0
ALAN MILLER	1992/93–1993/94	8	0
COLIN PATES	1989/90–1992/93	7	0
ADRIAN CLARKE	1994/95–1995/96	7	0
ALEXANDRE SONG	2005/06–PRESENT	7	0
NEIL HEANEY	1991/92–1993/94	6	0
GAVIN MCGOWAN	1992/93–1997/98	6	0
MATTHEW ROSE	1995/96–1996/97	5	0
PAOLO VERNAZZA	1997/98–2000/01	5	1
QUINCY OWUSU-ABEYIE	2003/04–2005/06	5	0
ALBERTO MENDEZ	1997/98–2001/02	4	0
RAMI SHAABAN	2002/03–2003/04	3	0
SEBASTIAN LARSSON	2004/05–2006/07	3	0
GRAHAM BARRETT	1999/2000–2002/03	2	0
TOMAS DANILEVICIUS	2000/01	2	0
KERREA GILBERT	2005/06–PRESENT	2	0
PERRY GROVES	1986/87–1992/93	1	0
LEE HARPER	1996/97	1	0
DAVID GRONDIN	1998/99–2002/03	1	0
FABIAN CABALLERO	1998/99	1	0
ISAIAH RANKIN	1996/97–1997/98	1	0
RHYS WESTON	1999/2000	1	0
JULIAN GRAY	1999/2000	1	0
BRIAN MCGOVERN	1999/2000	1	0
DAVID BENTLEY	2000/01–2005/06	1	0
TOMMY BLACK	1999/2000	1	0
RYAN GARRY	2002/03–PRESENT	1	0
STATHIS TAVLARIDIS	2001/02–2003/04	1	0
ARTURO LUPOLI	2004/05–2006/07	1	0
MART POOM	2005/06–2006/07	1	0

Adams, Tony 6, 9, 10–11, 21, 26, 34, 35, 70, 72, 76, 112, 115, 140, 156, 160, 166

Adebayor, Emmanuel 7, 115, 146–7

Africa Cup of Nations (2000) 68

Aliadiere, Jeremie 115, 122, 141

Almunia, Manuel 104, 115, 139

Anelka, Nicolas 7, 47, 66–7, 115, 122, 156

PFA Young Player of the Year award 62

Argentina 114

Arsenal Academy 18

Austria 115

Baptista, Julio 69, 158

Barrett, Graham 102, 115

Barthez, Fabien 34

Barton, Warren 91

Bartram, Vince 49

Bastin, Cliff 44

Belarus 115

Bellamy, Craig 125

Bendtner, Nicklas 141

Bentley, David 106, 141

Bergkamp, Dennis 7, 23, 34, 35, 46, 47, 55, 57, 59, 60 64, 97, 111, 115, 119, 120, 125, 136, 144, 162, awards 62, 63

Black, Tommy 111

Boa Morte, Luis 77, 115

Bould, Steve 6, 18–19, 21, 26, 35, 76, 141, 156, 160, 166

Brady, Liam 141, 156

Brazil 114

Bright, Mark 26

Bronckhorst, Giovanni van 115, 118

Caballero, Fabian 81, 114

Campbell, Kevin 20, 44, 46

Campbell, Sol 112, 116–17, 166

Cantona, Eric 151

Carter, Jimmy 42

Chapman, Herbert 166

Clarke, Adrian 57

Clichy, Gael 6, 115, 130, 157

club records 168–9

Cole, Andy 44

Cole, Ashley 87, 100–1, 125, 130, 141, 142, 157

Copa America (2004) 69

Court, David 141

Croatia 115

cult heroes 92–3

Cygan, Pascal 115, 123

Czech Republic 115

Danilevicius, Thomas 111, 115

Davis, Paul 9, 140

Denilson 7, 157, 158

Denmark 115

Diaby, Abou 7, 115, 151

Diawara, Kaba 91, 115

Dickov, Paul 50, 115

Dixon, Lee 6, 28–9, 32, 90, 112, 160

Djourou, Johan 6, 115, 134, 141

Donetsk, Shakhtar 16

Droboga, Didier 131

Dudek, Jerzy 136

Dunne, Richard 125

Eboue, Emmanuel 6, 112, 115, 142, 148

Edu 98–9, 114

European Championship (2000) 69

Fabregas, Francesc 7, 115, 136–7, 157, 159, 166, 169

FA Youth Cup 140

Flamini, Mathieu 115, 135

Flatts, Mark 48

Football Writers' Association Player of the Year 63

France 115

Gallas, William 115, 134, 154–5

Garde, Remi 59, 115

Garrincha 148

Garry, Ryan 111

Germany 115

Gilbert, Kerrea 129

Gilberto 7, 69, 114, 120–1, 157

Goal of the Season award 63

goals, scoring 100 22–3

Graham, George 6, 7, 9, 10, 14, 18, 28, 30, 40,
    44, 51, 53, 54, 55, 160–1, 162, 164
Gray, Julian 102
Greece 115
Grimandi, Gilles 72, 93, 115, 123
Grondin, David 81, 115
Groves, Perry 14, 92, 93
Guinea 115

Hapgood, Eddie 100
Harper, Lee 58
Hartson, John 53, 115, 156
Heaney, Neil 42, 140
Helder, Glenn 55, 115
Henry, Thierry 7, 35, 44, 47, 77, 78, 94 97, 100,
    104, 111, 112, 115, 119, 120, 122, 125,
    126, 158, 166
    awards 62–3
    departure 146
    European Championship (2000) 69
    invincible moment 124
    records 23, 169
    World Cup (1998) 68
High Five Matches 34–5
Hillier, David 27
Hleb, Alexandre 115, 126, 149
Holland 115
Houston, Stewart 164
Howard, Tim 110
Hoyte, Justin 6, 112, 141, 142
Hughes, Stephen 56, 140

invincible moments 124–5
Ireland 115
Italy 115
Ivory Coast 115

Jeffers, Francis 119
Jennings, Pat 30
Jensen, John 39, 92, 115

Kanu, Nwankwo 7, 77, 88–9, 111, 115, 119
Kennedy, Ray 156
Keown, Martin 6, 16–17, 76, 140, 157

Kiwomya, Chris 54

Larsson, Sebastian 115, 138, 141
Latvia 115
Lauren 90, 112–13, 115, 157
Lehmann, Jens 6, 104, 107, 115, 124, 125,
    132–3
Liberia 115
Limpar, Anders 6, 26, 35, 40–1, 115, 160
Linighan, Andy 26
Lithuania 115
Ljungberg, Fredrik 7, 34, 84–5, 104,
    115, 166
Lukic, John 15, 169
Lupoli, Arturo 115, 138, 141
Luzhny, Oleg 90, 115
Lydersen, Pal 43, 115

McGoldrick, Eddie 51
McGovern, Brian 102, 115
McGowan, Gavin 48
Malz, Stefan 91, 115
Manninger, Alex 82, 115
Marshall, Scott 50, 115
Marwood, Brian 32, 40, 160
Mendez, Alberto 80, 115
Merson, Paul 7, 12–13, 44, 140,
    156, 162
Miller, Alan 43
Minotti, Lorenzo 32
Morrow, Steve 38, 115
Morte, Luis Boa 6
Muamba, Fabrice 141

Neville, Gary 34
Northern Ireland 115
Norway 115

Okocha, Jay-Jay 124
O'Leary, David 8, 115
Olympic Games (2000) 68
Overmars, Marc 34, 36, 56, 59, 74, 78–9,
    115, 156, 166
Owusu-Abeyie, Quincy 115, 129

Parlour, Ray 7, 35, 36–7, 64, 156, 157, 169
Pates, Colin 21
Pennant, Jermaine 6, 96, 141, 169
perfect partnerships 46–7
Persie, Robin van 7, 47, 115, 138, 144–5, 158
Petit, Emmanuel 7, 34, 56, 64, 74–5, 78, 115, 118, 126, 166
PFA Fans Player of the Year 62–3
PFA Players' Player of the Year 62
PFA Young Player of the Year 62
Pires, Robert 7, 63, 100, 104–5, 115, 125, 144, 166, 169
Platt, David 7, 35, 63, 64–5, 162
Poom, Mart 158
Portugal 115

Radford, John 156
Rankin, Isaiah 83
Reyes, Jose Antonio 115, 125, 143
Rice, Pat 10, 165
Rioch, Bruce 36, 52, 55, 162–3
Rocastle, David 160
Ronaldo, Cristiano 136
Rose, Matthew 58, 140
Rosicky, Tomas 115, 150, 157

Sansom, Kenny 9, 24, 100
Schmeichel, Peter 34, 78, 84
Schwartz, Stefan 52, 115
Scotland 115
Seaman, David 6, 15, 26, 30–1, 49, 82, 107, 110, 132, 160
Selley, Ian 49
Senderos, Philippe 6, 115, 131, 134
Shaaban, Rami 115, 128
Shaw, Paul 57
Shearer, Alan 125
Silvinho 87, 114
Smith, Alan 22, 28, 32–3, 40, 44
Song, Alexandre 115, 158
Southall, Neville 35
Spain 115
Stepanovs, Igors 83, 115
Suker, Davor 77, 97, 115

Sweden 115
Switzerland 115

Tavlaridis, Stathis 115, 128
Taylor, Stuart 107, 141
teenage players 156–7
Thomas, Michael 15, 39
Togo 115
Toure, Kolo 6, 115, 123, 124, 126–7, 166

Ukraine 115
Upson, Matthew 6, 76, 156

Vaessen, Paul 156
Vernazza, Paolo 80
Vieira, Patrick 7, 56, 59, 64, 70–1, 74, 115, 120, 136, 151, 157, 166
Vivas, Nelson 86, 114

Walcott, Theo 7, 152–3, 157
Wales 115
Wenger, Arsène 6 10, 18, 24, 29, 36, 52, 63, 66, 70 74, 78, 94, 106, 126, 129, 134, 148, 156, 157, 158, 162, 166
Weston, Rhys 102, 115
Wilson, Bob 30
Wiltord, Sylvian 7, 34, 69, 104, 108–9, 111, 115, 119, 169
Winterburn, Nigel 6, 24–5, 87, 100
Woods, Chris 12
World Cup
    (1998) 68
    (2000) 69
Wreh, Christopher 73, 115
Wreh, George 73
Wright, Ian 7, 23, 32, 35, 40, 44–5, 46, 54, 66, 160
Wright, Richard 110

Youth Players 140–1

ACKNOWLEDGEMENTS

Executive Editor Trevor Davies
Editors Camilla Davis
Executive Art Editor Darren Southern
Designer Martin Topping, 'Ome Design
Picture Research Sophie Delpech
Senior Production Controller Martin Croshaw

Picture Acknowledgements

Action Images 15, 54; /Tony O'Brien 83, 131. **Arsenal Football Club** 6, 9, 13, 23 Top Right, 25, 26, 27, 29, 30, 31, 33, 37, 38, 42, 45, 48, 50, 50, 52, 53, 55, 56, 57, 59, 61, 68, 69, 69, 71, 72, 76, 77, 79, 82, 83, 85, 87, 89, 90, 91, 92, 93, 95, 96, 98, 100, 102, 105, 106, 109, 111, 117, 118, 119, 121, 122, 123, 127, 128, 128, 129, 129, 130, 132, 134, 135, 137, 138, 138, 139, 142, 143, 144, 146, 148, 149, 150, 153, 155, 158, 159, 168, 11, 17, 41, 57, 64, 80, 81, 107, 111, 113, 158, 164. **Colorsport** (Arsenal) 8, 14, 21, 42, 43, 43, 46, 49, 50, 75, 103, 51, 73; /Andrew Cowie 34, 39, 62, 63, 110, 125, 140, 141, 169;/ Kieran Galvin 141, 159;/ Mathew Impey 58;/ Nick Kidd 48;/ Paul Roberts 58; /Stuart Macfarlane 49, 86, 97, 140, 161, 163. **Getty Images** 20, 35, 47, 47, 102, 124, 125, 151, 157, 167, 169. **Offside**/David Davies 93; /Mark Leech 66. **PA Photos**/John Walton 103; /Neal Simpson 91; /Ross Kinnaird 22, 165; /Steve Morton 80; /Tony Marshall 81, 111.